Tear
Drenched
Nights

ויבכו העם בלילה ההוא
(במדבר יד:א).
אותה לילה ליל תשעה באב היה.
אמר להם הקדוש ברוך הוא
אתם בכיתם בכיה של חנם
ואני קובע לכם בכיה לדורות.
(תענית כט.)

The people cried on that night
(BeMidbar 14:1).
It was Tish'ah B'Av.
God said to them:
"On this night you cried
for no reason at all;
I will make this into
a night of tears
throughout your exile."
(Ta'anis 29a)

Tear Drenched Nights

TISH'AH B'AV:
THE TRAGIC LEGACY OF
THE MERAGLIM

MOSHE M. EISEMANN

Rabbi Moshe M. Eisemann
401 Yeshiva Lane, Apt. 3a
Baltimore, M.D. 21208
(410) 484-7396
www.yeshivakishiniev.org

Editor: Yacov David Shulman
Design: Misha Beletsky
Typography: Yehudit Massouda
Project Management: Nama Frenkel

This book was set in ITC Foundry Caslon 12 and Narkiss Classic

ISBN: 0-9769161-1-8

10 9 8 7 6 5 4 3 2 1

Distributed by:
Feldheim Publishers
POB 35002, Jerusalem, Israel 91350
200 Airport Executive Park, Nanuet, N.Y. 10954
www.feldheim.com

Printed in the USA

Contents

בס"ד

RABBI AHARON FELDMAN

ROSH HAYESHIVA

NER ISRAEL RABBINICAL COLLEGE

STUDY: 400 MT. WILSON LANE (410) 484-7200

RESIDENCE: 409 YESHIVA LANE (410) 653-9433

FAX (410) 484-3060

BALTIMORE, MARYLAND 21208

פורים דמוקפין תשס"ה

Rabbi Eisemann has deeply influenced the students at Ner Yisrael with his classes for over thirty years. It is therefore a matter of great joy for me to learn that he is now disseminating his teachings in book form when they will be available to the general public.

From the essays I have seen it is clear that they are inspiring and incisive in their analysis of their respective topics, as well as beautifully presented through elegant and masterful writing.

It is my hope that this book will be well received by all lovers of Torah learning and that it will be given all the recognition which it truly deserves.

With respects,

Aharon Feldman

Aharon Feldman
Rosh Yeshivas Ner Yisrael
Baltimore, MD

A Personal Note from the Author

Many years ago, I got involved in working to educate Jews from the Former Soviet Union through the Vaad Hatzolas Nidchei Yisroel. We discovered that in a residential day school, we could both educate and allow children to live as Jews full time. In 1990 Kishiniev Yeshiva was born.

We were given a building that used to be a synagogue. Before the Holocaust, the city of Kishiniev had 70 shuls, there were seforim published and there was even a Kishiniever Rebbe. Jews had been living there for centuries.

It's all gone now except for a few books, pictures and these few bright faces learning in our little Kishiniev Yeshiva.

It's a good school and I'm proud to be the "Rosh Yeshiva." As I write today in December, 2004, there are 40 boys and girls ages 12–17 in two small but comfortable buildings. We know today of 80 graduates of the Kishiniev Yeshiva, both men and women, who are living as proud and observant Jews. Some of them are married with children. Many are completing their education in the U. S. Some of them are teaching the next generation in the former Soviet Union. It's a small start and we would like to do more. However, it is costly work.

As a way of easing the burden, I came up with the idea of writing a series of simple, short books of Torah in the hopes that those who received them would help us. Many people have been generous, but the need continues.

I know there are many, many very important demands on you. I hope you will consider adding us to the list of the many projects you support. My address and phone number are listed below.

You can learn more about Kishiniev Yeshiva or donate online at www.kishinievyeshiva.org. On this site you can purchase many of my books. You can listen to or download tapes of classes I've given. We will be charging a modest fee for the books and the classes. We assure you, every penny you spend on our web site will benefit Kishiniev Yeshiva. Unlike a normal store, we will accept donations in excess of the "cost" of our products.

Rabbi Moshe Eisemann
401 Yeshiva Lane, Apt 3A
Baltimore, MD 21208
410-484-7396

www.kishinievyeshiva.org

This is the ninth book which I have sent out in as many years, in order to help with meeting the budget of the Yeshivah in Kishiniev. In a modest way, these books have become quite popular, which is of course gratifying.

For this book I have made a small change in style, which I want to explain to you.

In the earlier books I wrote in a kind of "yeshivishe" English, freely using Hebrew expressions as part of the text. There are, however, people who are not fluent Hebrew readers who have been frustrated by this intrusion of a second language. I have been asked a number of times to stick to English.

So, at the cost perhaps of losing a little "heimishkeit," I have eliminated the informal use of Hebrew. It now appears only in the form of longish quotes for which a translation or paraphrase is always provided.

I apologize to those of you who enjoyed the earlier, less formal style. Still, I am sure that it is a small sacrifice to make so that more people can enjoy the books.

Thanks to all of you.

Some Ruminations About Our History

I f you are about to embark upon this little book, you must be ready for some depressing reading. The episode of the spies, which from Chapter 5 onwards becomes the main focus of these essays, is not a happy one. Again and again, we will stand aghast at the sheer wrong-headedness of the choices that we made and the opportunities that we squandered. There will be some relief in the last chapter, but all in all we will leave the book with a feeling of history gone awry. We will be inclined to ask, as Eliyahu HaNavi was once asked in connection with a different major disappointment (see Yoma 19b at the bottom of the page), "What does—what can—the Ribbono shel Olam say when things go so dreadfully wrong?"

I will devote the rest of this essay to a search for what comfort we might find. I am writing these lines on the Fast of Gedaliah. Yesterday we read the *parashah* of Ha'azinu, which summons us to a sophisticated reading of history. Let us see whether we can develop a workable theory of Jewish history that will allow for all the disappointments.

The going will not be easy. But I hope that if you struggle on to the end, you will agree with me that it was worth the effort.

Here is a quote from Rambam (Hilchos Megillah 2:18):

כל ספרי הנביאים וכל הכתובים עתידין ליבטל לימות המשיח חוץ ממגילת אסתר הרי היא קיימת **כחמישה** חומשי תורה וכהלכות של תורה שבעל פה שאינן בטלין לעולם, ואע"פ שכל זכרון הצרות יבטל שנאמר, כי נשכחו הצרות הראשונות וכי נסתרו מעיני, ימי הפורים לא יבטלו שנאמר, וימי הפורים האלה לא יעברו מתוך היהודים וזכרם לא יסוף מזרעם.

All of NaCh—that is, Nevi'im and Kesuvim (the latter two-thirds of TaNaCh)—will cease to have relevance in the Messianic era. The only exception is the Book of Esther, which—in common with the five books of the Torah and the halachos of the oral Torah—will remain eternally valid. Although in the Messianic age there will be no reason to recall any of the earlier suffering . . . still, the celebration of Purim will not be curtailed. This, based upon the verse in the Book of Esther: *The celebration of these Purim days will never cease among the Jews; their memory will never be lost to the generations of the future.*

The concept that our NaCh is somehow time-bound is, of course, very strange to us.[1] Still, that is not the focus of our interest here. Here we want to understand the question implied in Rambam's words and what the answer might be.

Here is his question: *Although in the Messianic age there will be no reason to recall any of the earlier suffering . . . .* Rambam does not understand why the Book of Esther should outlast the rest of NaCh. It is at bottom no more than a story of suffering and salvation. Such stories abound in TaNaCh. Why should just this one remain of interest at a time when all suffering will have become a thing of the past?

2

Prologue

If this is the question, what is the answer? Rambam simply states the fact: *the celebration of Purim will not be curtailed.*

Well, why will it not?

The answer must be that the Book of Esther contains an immortal message, one that will remain fresh long after the details of the historical event have lost their claim upon our interest. Mordechai and Esther, Achashverosh and Haman—all these are a part of a story that in the Messianic era should be condemned to oblivion. There is only one actor in the drama Who is unshackled by the constraints of history—an actor Whose presence lingers on long after the others have made their exits. That is the actor Who never appears onstage and Who is therefore not hampered by the absence of a stage.

We have made some progress, but we still have a way to go. If all this is correct, why did Rambam not say something about it? He must have known that, as it stands, his statement leaves the reader with a question.

Why did Rambam not help us along?

I believe that Rambam did not owe us any explanation, because he had already presented us with the answer in the halachah immediately preceding this one. Let us take a look at Halachah 17:

מוטב לאדם להרבות במתנות אביונים מלהרבות בסעודתו ובשלוח
מנות לרעיו, שאין שם שמחה גדולה ומפוארה אלא לשמח לב עניים
ויתומים ואלמנות וגרים, שהמשמח לב האמללים האלו דומה לשכינה
שנאמר, להחיות רוח שפלים ולהחיות לב נדכאים.

It is better to spend much money on gifts to the poor than to spend it for one's own festive meal or on sending gifts to one's friends. This, because no celebration can match bringing joy to the poor, the orphans, the widows and the strangers. Whoever brings light into the lives of these unfortunates is acting *as the Ribbono shel Olam acts. As the verse states, [although God's abode is in the highest*

heavens, He chooses to be with the oppressed and the low-spir-
ited] in order to revive the spirits of the lowly and to bring life to
the hearts of the downtrodden.

Rambam is telling us some very basic truths, and we would be well advised to check our own Purim to see whether we have our priorities straight. Still, Rambam is not given to hyperbole, and we must try to understand what he means by saying that whoever acts in accordance with his prescription is *acting as the Ribbono shel Olam acts.* If he simply means to stress the importance of giving charity, we would have expected him to make this point in the halachos of charity. Why mention this idea in connection with the particular form of charity that we know as Mattanos LaEvyonim, the *gifts to the poor* of Purim?

The late, great Rav Yitzchak Hutner, *zatzal,* has some very profound thoughts on this passage. He believes that *acting as the Ribbono shel Olam acts* does not mean emulating God in His role as One Who cares profoundly about the poor, but emulating God in His role as the One Who brought about the miracle of Purim.

At the time of Purim, the Jewish people were profoundly depressed. They believed that the Ribbono shel Olam had given up on them.[2] The miracle of Purim, then, was God's own *gift to the poor* to his broken people. Their salvation told them that their relationship to the Ribbono shel Olam remained unimpaired, that the love binding them together had not become frayed. (See Rashi, Shabbos 88a, who uses the expression *me'ahavas hanes,* the love made manifest by means of the miracle.)

Rambam teaches us that he who makes gifts to the poor central to his Purim is *acting as the Ribbono shel Olam acts*—he is Godlike! God's Purim, too, centers upon the *gifts to the poor* which He gave his poor, broken, beloved people.

Purim is the day upon which the Ribbono shel Olam

4

wants us to emulate Him. He wants the lowly and the downtrodden to be on our minds.

When, therefore, Rambam tells us that of all NaCh, only the Book of Esther will continue to be read in the Messianic era, it is, in the light of what we have now learned from the halachah immediately preceding this one, self-explanatory. Even in those heady days, when all the suffering of the past will have been forgotten, we will still need to know the Ribbono shel Olam (to the extent that it is given us to know Him). The Book of Esther will forever be our text for meeting the Ribbono shel Olam as the One Whose main concern is *to revive the spirits of the lowly and to bring life to the hearts of the downtrodden.*

We will now take these thoughts a little further. As long as we are studying Rambam's Hilchos Megillah, we should give some more thought to the way he words his assertion concerning the Book of Esther. He writes: *The Book of Esther, in common with the five books of the Torah and the halachos of the oral Torah, will remain eternally valid.*[3] What does Rambam wish to clarify with these comparisons? Why not state simply that the Book of Esther will remain eternally valid?[4]

It has been suggested that Rambam is making the point that the Book of Esther, besides being a part of NaCh, is also a discrete entity with its own unique character. The Book refers to itself as *divrey shalom ve'emes*, words of peace and truth (Esther 9:30). The Yerushalmi (Megilah 1:5) connects that *truth* to the verse *Do not sell a truth once acquired* (Mishley 23:23), which of course refers to the Torah. The Yerushalmi concludes that this association tells us that the Book of Esther contains a truth that is *similar to the truth of the Torah.*[5]

It is therefore possible that Rambam is offering a technical explanation for the resilience of the Book of Esther.

It is judged by unique standards because it is unique. Its similarity to *the truth of the Torah* determines that just as the five books of the Torah will continue to be read and learned in the Messianic era, so will the Book of Esther. [6]

This essay is certainly not the place to deal with all the issues raised by these rather arcane ideas. I recommend that the interested reader follow up in the sources which I cite in endnote 6. Here my focus is as follows: I would like to understand what makes the Book of Esther into a kind of mini-Torah. What is that *truth* that the Book asserts for itself, a truth qualitatively different from the truth to which all the other books of NaCh can certainly lay claim? It seems that not all truths are equal.

That is precisely true. Not all truths are equal. Let us spend a few moments studying Rambam, Hilchos Yesodey HaTorah 1:3–4.

ג. ואם יעלה על הדעת שאין כל הנמצאים מלבדו מצויים הוא לבדו יהיה מצוי, ולא יבטל הוא לבטולם, שכל הנמצאים צריכין לו והוא ברוך הוא אינו צריך להם ולא לאחד מהם, לפיכך אין אמתתו כאמתת אחד מהם.

ד. הוא שהנביא אומר וה׳ אלהים אמת, הוא לבדו האמת ואין לאחר אמת כאמתתו, והוא שהתורה אומרת אין עוד מלבדו, כלומר אין שם מצוי אמת מלבדו כמותו.

3. If we could imagine that the entire universe ceased to exist, He alone would still exist. The absence of everything else could never impugn His Presence. This is so because all that exist need Him, but He needs none of them. Accordingly, we conclude that His truth is in no way comparable to theirs.

4. Yirmeyahu had this in mind when he said that HaShem is the true God. Only He is "true" in the sense that the word "truth" is applicable here. None other shares this "truth." The Torah has this in mind when it proclaims, *There is none besides Him!* This means that there is none besides Him who compares to His "truth."

Prologue

I believe that this passage is the key to understanding the unique truth that is shared only by the five books of the Torah and the Book of Esther. We will have to take things slowly. First we will think about the Torah and only then move on to the Book of Esther.

So what is the unique *truth of the Torah*?

Ramban, in his Introduction to Sefer BeReishis, can help. Here is a short quote from a long and complex section:

עוד יש בידינו קבלה של אמת כי כל התורה כולה שמותיו של הקב"ה
שהתיבות מתחלקות לשמות בענין אחד כאילו תחשוב על דרך משל
כי פסוק בראשית יתחלק לתיבות אחרות כגון בראש יתברא אלהים
וכל התורה כן.

We have a reliable tradition that the entire text of the Torah consists of "Names" describing the Ribbono shel Olam. This is possible because we are able to parse sentences and phrases differently than does our tradition. Let us take the first phrase in Chumash as an example. The words *BeReishis bara Elokim* can be divided so as to read *Berosh yisbara Elokim*. It is possible to make similar adjustments throughout the Torah.

If we consider this statement together with Rambam's words that we quoted earlier, I believe that we can put our finger on the unique truth that expresses itself in the five books of the Torah. The Ribbono shel Olam is uniquely True, and the Torah is, at one level, a collection of the Ribbono shel Olam's Names. It follows that the Torah is uniquely "true."

To apply the same logic to the Book of Esther, we will have to make a daring leap. I offer the following as no more than a suggestion. We all know that the Name of the Ribbono shel Olam is not mentioned in the Book of Esther. We have all certainly wondered why and probably have come across a number of different explanations. I will add one more to this list. The entire Book is a Name of the Ribbono shel Olam. No formal name needs to appear, because every word announces the Ribbono shel Olam as One Whose interest lies in *reviving the spirits of the lowly and bringing life to the hearts of the downtrodden.* Every letter has to be written with all the attention to detail that one would lavish on writing a Torah scroll, because the Book of Esther shares with the Torah scroll the distinction of being a projection of the Ribbono shel Olam. The Torah scroll does this by providing us with a versatile text. The Book of Esther does the same by telling us a story. It contains the same truth that is to be found in the Torah scroll.

God appears to us in many different roles. The Book of Esther projects Him as the One Who glories in the role of *reviving the spirits of the lowly and bringing life to the hearts of the downtrodden.* God is determined that this is how we should know Him and experience Him forever and ever. Megillas Esther must never and will never be forgotten.

We have called this book about the Meraglim *Tear-Drenched Nights.* We all know the Gemara from Ta'anis 29a:

אמר רבה אמר רבי יוחנן אותה לילה ליל תשעה באב היה. אמר להם הקדוש ברוך הוא, אתם בכיתם בכיה של חנם ואני קובע לכם בכיה לדורות.

Rabbah taught in the name of R. Yochanan: That night [when the people wept at the report the Meraglim had brought back] was Tish'ah B'Av, *the ninth of Av.* God said to them: "On this night you cried for no reason at all; I will make this into a night of tears throughout your exile."

8

Prologue

We do not know when it will all end. There have been so many, many tears on so many, many nights. One day we will understand it all. In the meantime we have much to do to better ourselves, to educate our children, to create caring and holy families, caring and holy communities—in short, to ready ourselves to meet the King.

All this has prodded me insistently to do some careful thinking about our history. Let me share one of my perplexities with you.

Our Sages teach us that after the Ribbono shel Olam had created many different worlds, none of which gave Him satisfaction, He made this one and said, "This is the one that pleases Me." I am plagued by a nagging uncertainty. Would He still say the same today? The world has changed radically for the worse from the one that appears to have been originally planned. Can it be that it still gives the Ribbono shel Olam pleasure?

Let us make an accounting and see what we humans have wrought. The following list is of course incomplete. There are countless other derelictions that could have been included.

1. When God created man, He placed him in Gan Eden. It was within such perfection that He wanted us to live. But when Adam sinned, life moved into an angry and recalcitrant environment. The lion's share of his life was now to be spent in fighting a sullen, uncooperative earth. It would be hard to imagine a more radical departure from the ideal.

2. The experiment begun with Adam did not work. Ten generations had to be wiped out in order to make a fresh beginning possible. Even No'ach was spared only as a *gift not really deserved*.[7] The Flood came about because of another dreadful regression. God determined to send the Flood only after He had seen that mankind had sunk to a level where man *is just flesh* (BeReishis 6:3). Ramban

explains that this phrase describes a brute whose physicality predominates over his spirituality. Even No'ach, whose task it became to father a new humanity, was, in the end, a *man of the field* (BeReishis 9:20). The human race had irredeemably turned into something very different from that which the Ribbono shel Olam had had in mind.

3. The generation of the Tower of Babel changed human society forever. There had been no original intent to divide mankind into nations.[8] The ideal state is the one in which *there is one nation, all of whose members share the same language.* But in their perversity, these people turned the ideal on its head and allowed it to inveigle them into a rebellion against God. History took a sharp turn, and instead of recording the glorious story of united humanity, it gets its hands dirty in recording the depressing futilities of the eternal bickering between nations that has made our world into such a depressing place. The need for Klal Yisrael as a Chosen People has its genesis in the generation of the Tower of Babel.

4. There was a moment of hope when, at the foot of Mount Sinai, we reached the level that the Ribbono shel Olam had had in mind for us (Shabbos 164a). But this lasted only forty days. The episode of the golden calf then shifted us from the first set of Tablets of the Law to the second, from a level of Torah study at which we would have become so identified with the Torah[9] that we would never have forgotten any of it (Eiruvin 54a) to one in which we know only too well how tenuous is our grasp, how weak our hold, how easily our knowledge all slips away.[10]

5. There is a view (see, for example, Sforno on Shemos 20:21) that if not for the episode of the golden calf, there would have been no need for a central Mishkan (the Sanctuary in the desert) and later, a Beis HaMikdash. Instead, the norm would have been, *Wherever I make My Name known, I will come to you and bless you* (Shemos 20:21).

Prologue

Every home would have been a Beis HaMikdash, every first-born son a Kohen. We suffered a precipitous descent indeed!

6. From the episode of the golden calf we move on to the episode of the spies, to the study of which this book is devoted. As we move through chapter after depressing chapter, we will learn of the horrors that this event left in its wake. The entire gamut of our dreadful, alienated, unhallowed exile finds its source in that sad failure to measure up.

What we have said above is true, is it not? One imperfection follows the other with disheartening regularity. Once more we should ask the question that we raised earlier. Is it possible that, after all this, the Ribbono shel Olam would still say that this world pleases Him? Or is the Ribbono shel Olam doomed to be disappointed in the work upon which He lavished so much care and love?

I believe that the first part of this essay can help answer this question. It is specifically in an imperfect world that the Presence of the Ribbono shel Olam, in His capacity to revive the spirit of the lowly and the heart of the downtrodden, shines most brightly. We have created a world for ourselves in which we stagger around, lowly and downtrodden. But the Ribbono shel Olam continues to be with us; He never loses patience. No matter how far we may fall, we are never so low that He ceases to care for us. That, indeed, is a world concerning which the Ribbono shel Olam can say, *This is the one that pleases Me.*

Why? Why does the Ribbono shel Olam not give up on us?

I think that the Ribbono shel Olam would give an answer which might be formulated along the following lines:

"Do not try too hard to understand Me. My thoughts are not yours. Do not be overly concerned. You are happy when things go well, but I am happy when I am able to revive the lowly of spirit and the downtrodden. I have My own ideas about history. Do not worry. In the end, you too will understand."

Armed, now, with faith and hope, let us begin our journey.

We have become experts at *galus* living. Two thousand years away from home leave their mark. We have only memories, and memory is treacherous. We block, we color, we edit and, in the end, we invent. The past is not only hazy but distorted.

And yet . . . and yet, against all logic, the Torah seems not only to trust our memories but even commands us to remember. "Remember how you left Egypt!" "Remember what Amalek did to you!" "Remember how you once stood at Sinai!" "Remember how you constantly angered God in the wilderness!" The Ribbono shel Olam knows how all-too-human we are, knows how flawed and inexact our recollections will be, and still He bids us make our pasts players in our present and our future. He seems to be telling us that even if we will not get it all straight, it is still better than nothing. Even a flawed recollection can do important work.

Here is a story of remembering.

The Levi'im sitting mutely on the banks of Babylon's rivers understood that an aberrant exile must stifle the harmonies welling up from within the Jewish soul. They refused to allow their fingers to strum their harps once the flow from heart to hand had been broken. They could not nor would they attempt to sing the "song of HaShem" on foreign soil. But each one of them[1] was determined to keep his memories alive.

אם אשכחך ירושלם תשכח ימיני

תדבק לשוני לחכי אם לא אזכרכי...

If I forget you, Yerushalayim, may my right hand wither,[2]

May my tongue cleave to my palate if I do not speak of you[3]...(Tehillim 137:5-6).

What was it that they promised never to forget? Was it the old glory or the smoldering ruins? Rashi tells us that they would never forget the destroyed Yerushalayim, nor would they ever stop mourning for it. He has opted for the latter of our two suggestions.

And yet, I wonder whether the context does not favor the former. The Levi'im had just refused to play their beloved music for the amusement of their captors. Would, then, the sacred music be forgotten through disuse? The answer, if I am correct, is sharp and clear. Their harps would remain silent, but Yerushalayim would remain alive in the memory of the Levi'im. The holy music would continue to reverberate in their hearts.

It all seems so simple. So why did our Sages reject this option? Surely the pain of our bereavement would be sharpened if we had a clearer image of what it was that we lost. Would the picture of the mute harps hanging accusingly from the reeds in the river not have wrenched our hearts the more if we had remembered the tunes which had once set them to dancing?

Our memories of the first Beis HaMikdash are of unmitigated sorrow. We have no fewer than four fast days to commemorate various stages of the Destruction,[4] yet no commemoration at all which might keep alive for us the unbounded joy of Shlomo HaMelech's inauguration of the Beis HaMikdash. Why should this be so? Does that supreme moment, the unparalleled pinnacle of Jewish achievement,[5] not deserve to be somehow immortalized?

It is almost as though the destruction of the Beis HaMikdash defines not only itself but also, retroactively, the years during which it flourished. The flames that consumed it cast a long shadow backwards over even the years of its glory. Something, then, was terribly wrong from the very beginning. The Beis HaMikdash itself was somehow flawed and carried the seed of its destruction within itself.

Come, let us try to learn something of this sad story.

I.

Missed

Opportunities

The Beis HaMikdash was conceived in sorrow. It should not have been so. It need not have been so. But we were small when we might have been great, were apathetic when the dream of the Divine Presence among us should have galvanized us to determined action. History called and there was no one at home. We were busy with the present and did not have the spiritual energy to dream.

It all started with an episode which must be one of the most mysterious in TaNaCh. I refer to David HaMelech's tragic decision to take a census of the people. He was wrong.[1] He brought untold suffering to his people.[2] They died in their thousands in a plague that was sent as direct punishment for what David had done.[3]

Why would David HaMelech have made such an egregious error?

Here is the introductory verse to this episode from II Shmuel 24:1.

ויסף אף ידוד לחרות בישראל ויסת את דוד בהם לאמר לך מנה את
ישראל ואת יהודה.

1. Missed Opportunities

Once more HaShem showed anger against Yisrael, inciting David against them, saying, "Go, take a census of Yisrael and Yehudah."[4]

Here we have it. The Ribbono shel Olam wanted this to happen. He actually *incited* David to do what he normally would not have done. Moreover, He incited David *against Yisrael*.

What can this possibly mean? How are we to understand that the Ribbono shel Olam would goad anyone, let alone David HaMelech, to sin? And why incite him *against Yisrael*?

Ramban will help us understand. His explanation derives from the fact that the plague and its aftermath led directly to the discovery of the site of the Beis HaMikdash.

This is how it happened. The Ribbono shel Olam sent an angel to spread the plague in Yerushalayim. This angel, evidently an angel of mercy, went straight to Mount Moriah in the hope that the memory of the *akeidah*, the sacrifice of Yitzchak, might elicit God's forgiveness. That is exactly what happened. God called to the angel, "Enough! The time has come to draw back."

David then erected an altar and sacrificed upon it. The Ribbono shel Olam sent down a heavenly fire to consume the sacrifice. By doing so, He indicated that all was now well. David took this as a sign that the altar marked the site upon which the Beis HaMikdash was to be built.

So much for background; now to Ramban. The relevant passage is to be found at BeMidbar 16:21.

. . . ואני אומר בדרך סברא, שהיה עונש על ישראל בהתאחר בנין בית הבחירה, שהיה הארון הולך מאהל אל אהל כגר בארץ ואין השבטים מתעוררים לאמר נדרוש את ה' ונבנה הבית לשמו, כענין שנאמר (דברים יב ה) לשכנו תדרשו ובאת שמה, עד שנתעורר דוד לדבר

17

מימים רבים ולזמן ארוך . . . והנה דוד מנעו השם יתברך מפני שאמר
(דה"י א כב ח) כי דמים רבים שפכת ארצה לפני, ונתאחר עוד הבנין
עד מלוך שלמה. ואלו היו ישראל חפצים בדבר ונתעוררו בו מתחלה
היה נעשה בימי אחד מהשופטים או בימי שאול, או גם בימי דוד, כי
אם שבטי ישראל היו מתעוררים בדבר לא היה הוא הבונה אבל ישראל
הם היו הבונים. אבל כאשר העם לא השגיחו, ודוד הוא המשגיח
והמתעורר והוא אשר הכין הכל היה הוא הבונה, והוא איש משפט
ומחזיק במדת הדין ולא הוכשר בבית הרחמים, ועל כן נתאחר הבנין כל
ימי דוד בפשיעת ישראל. ועל כן היה הקצף עליהם. ועל כן היה המקום
אשר יבחר ה' לשום שמו שם נודע בענשם ובמגפתם.

I suggest that Israel deserved to be punished, because
their negligence had delayed the building of the Beis
HaMikdash much longer than was necessary. It could
have been built any time after Klal Yisrael entered Eretz
Yisrael. They were at fault because during all these years
they made no move to start the process. Apparently, it
simply did not occur to them to do so. In the end, David
himself broached the subject. However, he was disqualified by God because of the lives that he had taken
in battle.

Now if the idea had come from the people, David
would never have been excluded from the project. His
personal standing would have been irrelevant, since he
would simply have been serving as their surrogate. It
was only because he and not they took the initiative that
the blood which he had shed in his many wars stood in
the way. The fact that he took the initiative would make
the Beis HaMikdash "his." This the Ribbono shel Olam
did not want.

It was the people's laxity that turned God against
them.

The result of all this was that the location of the Beis
HaMikdash was revealed in consequence of the plague
that they had suffered.

1. Missed Opportunities

From the very beginning, a shadow hung over Shlomo HaMelech's Beis HaMikdash. The plague was bad enough. Worse still, much worse, was the lethargy that the people displayed towards the idea of a Beis HaMikdash in their midst. They were not tantalized by the Ribbono shel Olam's promise that He would dwell among them. They were perfectly happy to leave things as they had always been. They failed to understand the passion expressed in Tehillim 42:3: *My soul thirsts for God, the living God; I thirst for the time when I will be able to enter the Presence of the Ribbono shel Olam.*

Things started off on the wrong foot. Other mistakes would be made. It is not a happy story, but one we must learn. We cannot correct our errors if we will not face them.

We have much to learn. Let us soldier on.

2.

Another
Miscalculation

Expressions that people use, and certainly expressions employed by our Sages, do not just happen. However, the original connection between words and the reality that they represent has often been sucked into one of the "black holes" of the passing centuries. Still, we can try and must hope that we hit reasonably close to the mark in deciphering these terms.

Throughout the Talmud and the Midrashim, the Beis HaMikdash is called *Beis Olamim*. I suspect that this expression finds its source in the opening sentence of Shlomo HaMelech's inaugural prayer (I Melachim 8:13), *I have built a habitation for You where You will be firmly [olamim] ensconced.* Still, this provides only a source but not a meaning. What precisely does this name convey?[1] *Olam* can mean either *world* or *eternity.* Which of the two is meant here? Do we mean *a habitation that will continue to all eternity*[2] or *a habitation belonging to more than one world*?

The Talmud (Menachos 29b) seems to favor the latter interpretation. A verse states: *Trust in HaShem forever, for HaShem is a Rock that is* olamim (Yeshayahu 24:6). The Talmud explains that *he who puts his trust in the Ribbono shel Olam will be rewarded. God will be his refuge in both this world [olam] and the next.*[3]

If we are correct, then *olamim* is an *abode that exists in more than one world.* What might this mean?

We need to take a look at Chagigah 12b, where the Talmud discusses a number of names that occur in TaNaCh, all of which refer to what we would call "heaven." The passage concludes that there are in fact a number of different "heavens," each with its own nature or function. One of these is *Zevul.* This is what the Talmud suggests:

זבול שבו ירושלים ובית המקדש, ומזבח בנוי, ומיכאל השר הגדול עומד ומקריב עליו קרבן, שנאמר, בנה בניתי בית זבל לך מכון לשבתך עולמים.

[One of these names is] *Zevul.* This is where Yerusha-layim, the Beis HaMikdash and the altar are located. It is where the archangel Michael sacrifices upon the altar. It is this which Shlomo HaMelech referred to when, in his inaugural prayer, he said, *I have built a House that parallels the one situated in Zevul.* [Instead of translating *zevul* as *habitation,* the Talmud takes it as a proper name.]

Apparently, the Beis HaMikdash, the *Beis Olamim,* is the incarnation of an idea that has its real place among the heavens. There is a divine blueprint which served as inspiration and guide to Shlomo HaMelech when he constructed his Beis HaMikdash.

Did he succeed? Was his Beis HaMikdash a true rendering of the Ribbono shel Olam's intent? It would seem that it was not. Surely one of the properties of the non-physical Beis HaMikdash in Zevul is indestructibility. Safely located in the heavens, it is not vulnerable to attack. When Nevuchadnetzar put Shlomo's Beis HaMikdash to the flames, it became clear that this was not the Beis HaMikdash that God had intended. Something from the very start had been wrong.

What was that?

Here is Sforno's thinking in his remarks to Shemos 38:22:

ובצלאל בן אורי בן חור למטה יהודה עשה, שהיו ראשי אומני מלאכת המשכן וכליו מיוחסים וצדיקים שבדור, ובכן שרתה שכינה במעשה ידיהם ולא נפל ביד האויבים, אבל מקדש שלמה שהיו עושי המלאכה בו מצור, אע"פ ששרתה בו שכינה נפסדו חלקיו והוצרך לחזק בדק הבית ונפל בסוף הכל ביד אויבים, אבל בית שני שלא היה בו גם אחד מכל אלה התנאים לא שרתה בו השכינה, ונפל ביד אויבים. . . .

The Mishkan, in contrast to Shlomo HaMelech's Beis HaMikdash, was never destroyed. It became a true and permanent home to God's Presence because Betzalel and Uri were not only great tzaddikim but also of perfect lineage, scions of God's Chosen People.

The Beis HaMikdash was different. It was vulnerable to the ravages of time, requiring constant care and repair, and it was ultimately destroyed. It is true that there too God's Presence dwelt, but the quality of permanence escaped it. It was built by non-Jewish workers sent to Shlomo from Tyre.

David HaMelech had articulated his vision of the Beis HaMikdash that Shlomo was to build. It was to be a huge building of surpassing beauty, one that would be admired throughout the world (I Divrey HaYamim 22:5). Shlomo invited Chiram of Tyre to join him in building this House of God, because this would assure him of the most skillful and accomplished artisans. The situation seemed to demand this move, and Shlomo made it in good conscience. There is certainly nothing in the Torah to suggest that non-Jews are disqualified from building the Beis HaMikdash.

Nevertheless, if Sforno is right, Shlomo HaMelech was wrong. No halachah was contravened, but the spirit in which we are bidden to welcome the Ribbono shel Olam into our midst was offended.

2. Another Miscalculation

We need to analyze this a little further. Let us leave that for the next chapter.

3.

Building
a Sanctuary

Halachos are what Jews "do." Customs—
minhagim—are the showcase for what Jews
"feel." Jewish customs are windows upon the
Jewish soul.

Here is a custom with which most of us are familiar. It
is a simple, undemanding gesture, but it moves us with
its simple rightness.

In Ashkenazic households, it has become the custom
to place a special goblet upon the Seder table. It is known
as *Eliyahu's cup*. It is a well-loved symbol of hope and anticipation. The contemplation of our past to which we
devote the first part of the Seder gives way to a real and
urgent longing for the promised future. On this of all
nights, we want Eliyahu with us.

Who gets to pour this cup of welcome? In most households, it is the host who does the honors. For the rest of
the Seder, it is instead the host who gets served. The free-
dom that we celebrate this night comes wrapped in privi-
lege. But this goblet is different. One does not delegate
the welcoming of a treasured guest.

Back, now, to the previous chapter, where we promised
to revisit the implications of co-opting the Tyrian

artisans into the building of the Beis HaMikdash. They were certainly the best that could be had, and their efforts produced a building which was much grander than anything that the Jews, left to their own devices, could have produced. Why, then, must this seemingly sensible move be considered so misguided?

We could simply accept that this was the story of Eliyahu's cup all over again. On Seder night, Jewish sensibilities would be offended were the host to delegate the welcoming of Eliyahu to others. Similarly, it stands to reason that delegating to non-Jewish workers the building of the Beis HaMikdash—the guest room for the Shechinah—was a grievous fault.

However, things are not quite so simple. It is one thing to expect the simple decencies, but it is quite another to view such a dereliction as sufficiently heinous to lead to the destruction of the Beis HaMikdash.

So we will have to search a little further.[1]

It seems to me that, if we are to grasp the full implications of Sforno's contention, we must go to Moshe Rabbeinu's Mishkan.

Here is a quote from Rashi on Pekudey 39:33.

ויביאו את המשכן וגו'. שלא היו יכולין להקימו, ולפי שלא עשה משה שום מלאכה במשכן, הניח לו הקדוש ברוך הוא הקמתו, שלא היה יכול להקימו שום אדם מחמת כובד הקרשים, שאין כח באדם לזקפן, ומשה העמידו. אמר משה לפני הקדוש ברוך הוא איך אפשר הקמתו על ידי אדם, אמר לו עסוק אתה בידך נראה כמקימו, והוא נזקף וקם מאליו, וזהו שנאמר (שמות מ יז) הוקם המשכן, הוקם מאליו. מדרש רבי תנחומא.

[After all the components of the Mishkan had been completed, the people brought everything to Moshe. Rashi tackles the question: Why? Why could not the same artisans who had manufactured the various parts raise the Mishkan up as well? Rashi answers as follows:

They brought the Mishkan to Moshe] because they themselves were unable to raise it. [How did this come about? It was] because up to this point, Moshe had in no way taken part in the creation of the Mishkan. Therefore, the Ribbono shel Olam reserved the raising of the Mishkan for him. He made sure that no one else would be able to raise the beams and that it would therefore devolve upon Moshe to do it.

Moshe asked the Ribbono shel Olam, "How can any one person raise this huge structure?"

God answered him, "You make the effort and it will stand up by itself. It will only appear as though you have raised it."

There is much in this Midrash which should engage our attention.[2] However, in order to keep an inordinately complex subject as simple as possible, we will deal only with the part which impacts directly upon our thinking in this essay.

Here is what we need to understand. Moshe Rabbeinu realizes that it is up to him to set up the Mishkan. He feels that it is a task which is physically beyond him; the beams are just too heavy. The Ribbono shel Olam assures him that this will present no problem. Moshe has only to go through the motions. The Ribbono shel Olam Himself will do the actual raising. Thus the Midrash. Now for our problem. What is the point of this charade? Why make it appear as though Moshe Rabbeinu is raising the Mishkan when in fact he is not?

It is, of course, not a charade at all. It is, on the contrary, the unadorned reality of what happens when the Ribbono shel Olam desires to find a dwelling place on earth.[3]

Here is what He says to us: "My children! I long to have a Presence among you because I know that such a Presence will elevate your lives, fill them with joy and fulfillment, and consummate the pact which we made at Sinai. But here's the rub. You cannot bring Me down; the distance between us is too great. However, I will come of My own accord. But I will do so only in response to your efforts to make Me welcome. Do your bit and I will do Mine. Strain at raising the impossible beams and you will suddenly find them easy to lift. Bring your sacrifices upon the altar that you will build for Me and My heavenly fire will come down to consume them. Desire Me and you shall have Me."

Viewed from this standpoint, the importation of foreign labor to produce a building of surpassing magnificence is indeed an aberration. It focuses upon house rather than home, opts for outer beauty to the detriment of inner coherence and integrity. How welcome can the Ribbono shel Olam feel in the most gorgeous of chambers when these have been wrought by uncaring, crass, obtuse artisans from Tyre? Can such a soulless museum impel a loving Father to gather His children in His ample embrace?

How could Shlomo HaMelech have erred so tragically? We try to tackle this important question at the end of the next chapter. In the meantime, we have some other leads to follow.

4.

Somber

Intimations

Neither joy nor sorrow is reticent. A sunny disposition expresses itself in a cheerful bearing (Mishley 15:13), and Kain's bitter disillusionment was registered on his face for all to see (BeReishis 4:6). Still, we speak approvingly of a person of whom it can be said that *he keeps his sorrow to himself and manages to maintain an appearance of unclouded serenity.*[1]

How did Shlomo HaMelech appear during the ecstatic inaugural celebrations that marked the completion of the Beis HaMikdash? It had taken seven long years (I Melachim 6:38), but now the waiting was over. At last the Jews were able to bring the Ark from its temporary quarters and install it lovingly in the Holy of Holies. They were not disappointed. As the Kohanim left, the holy Presence of the Ribbono shel Olam, manifest in a dense cloud, filled the House of HaShem (8:10).

All seemed to be well, and the celebrations that followed were everything that one might have expected on such a momentous occasion.

But all was *not* well, and if Shlomo's face did not betray the pain in his heart, we must nevertheless take it for granted that his happiness was tinged by profound sorrow.[2]

Here is a quote from Rambam, Hilchos Beis Ha-Bechirah 4:1.

אבן היתה בקדש הקדשים במערבו שעליה היה הארון מונח, ולפניו צנצנת המן ומטה אהרן, ובעת שבנה שלמה את הבית וידע שסופו ליחרב בנה בו מקום לגנוז בו הארון למטה במטמוניות עמוקות ועקלקלות ויאשיהו המלך צוה וגנזו במקום שבנה שלמה....

There was a stone in the west of the Holy of Holies upon which the Ark lay. . . . Now when Shlomo built the Beis HaMikdash *and knew that it was destined to be destroyed*,[3] he built a hiding place for the Ark deep down in subterranean passageways. Later on, Yoshiyahu hid the Ark in the place that Shlomo had prepared.

There we have it. All along, even while the foundations of the Beis HaMikdash were still being dug, Shlomo HaMelech carried a dreadful truth in his heart: It would not last. The time would come when the Divine Presence, now being welcomed so joyously into their midst, would depart.[4] The Beis HaMikdash would become just a pretentious building without any lasting significance. It would be nothing more than a mockery of the glory that it had known. It would crumble before the onslaught of any enemy strong enough to destroy it. A dark, malevolent presence was casting a shadow over the celebrants. What terrible knowledge to carry in one's breast!

What was the reason? Why was the Beis HaMikdash, so earnestly and altruistically conceived by David Ha-Melech, so meticulously and conscientiously brought to completion by Shlomo, doomed to destruction?

My good friend R. Yehudah Copperman of Yerusha-layim has directed me to two relevant comments in Sforno's work on the Chumash.

The first comment is on BeMidbar 14:28. Here is the background: After the spies return with their negative report, the people panic and, in their terror, they express the fear that if they attempt to enter the land, all manner of dreadful things will happen. Among them, *Our wives and our children will be taken as booty* (BeMidbar 14:3). Our verse is God's response to their hysteria. He affirms that everything which they fear will indeed come about, although not in the way that they have anticipated. They fear that these horrors will be a result of listening to God. They are wrong. They will come about because of a lack of belief in God's benevolence. Here is what God says: *Tell them this: As I live—the words of HaShem—I shall do precisely as you have spoken . . . [also concerning what you feared that] your children will be taken as booty [that is going to happen]*.

To this, Sforno remarks: [These things will indeed happen, but they will occur] at different times in their history. With these words God swore an oath. It is to this oath that the Psalmist refers in Psalm 106:26 where he says, *He swore that he would destroy them in the wilderness* and CAST THEIR CHILDREN INTO EXILE AMONG THE NATIONS. Yechezkel, too, makes reference to this oath when he says (20:23), *I raised My hands in an oath while they were in the desert,* TO SCATTER THEM AMONG THE NATIONS.

Sforno asserts that the Psalmist and Yechezkel are in agreement concerning the meaning of the passage in BeMidbar. As a direct result of the debacle of the spies, Jews would one day have to go into exile among the nations. As he reads God's oath, it does indeed transpire that the destruction of Shlomo's Beis HaMikdash was a foregone conclusion.

Sforno's understanding of the BeMidbar passage forms the background to his commentary on Devarim 3: 25–26. Moshe Rabbeinu has been told that he will die in the wilderness and so will not lead the Israelites into the

Promised Land. He prays to God, asking Him to reconsider.

Here is Sforno's commentary on these verses:

אעברה נא

Let me now cross
So that I can destroy *all* the inhabitants of Canaan, thus guaranteeing that Israel will never be exiled from the land.

ואראה את הארץ הטובה

and see the good land
I will make the land "good" with the blessing that I will give it, so that it will be "good" for Israel for all generations.

ויתעבר ה׳ בי למענכם.

But HaShem became angry with me because of you.
Because it was my wish that the land should be yours forever, that you would never be exiled from it. He, however, had already sworn *to scatter your children among the nations.*

We may formulate Sforno's thesis as follows: Had Moshe Rabbeinu been permitted to enter Eretz Yisrael, no exile would ever have been possible. But that could not be permitted. God's oath, taken at the time of the spies, guaranteed that Shlomo HaMelech's Beis HaMikdash would not last and that the people would be dragged into *galus.* Shlomo HaMelech knew well what he was doing when from the very beginning he made provisions for the inevitable undoing of all his efforts.

At the end of the last chapter, we wondered how Shlomo HaMelech could have made the error of inviting Chiram to help him in erecting the Beis HaMikdash. Perhaps it was no error at all. Perhaps we have our causes and consequences backwards. Perhaps he used Chiram precisely because he knew that his Beis HaMikdash was not fated to stand forever.[5]

5.

The Episode
of the
Spies Revisited

I n the last chapter, we followed Sforno's serpentine
travels through the sources. These prompted him
to assert that it was already a foregone conclusion
from the time of the spies that Shlomo HaMelech's Beis
HaMikdash would in the end be destroyed.[1]

Sforno's thesis is foreshadowed in the Talmud. The
relevant passage will prove to be a fertile source for de-
veloping a breathtakingly innovative theory concerning
the relationship between Klal Yisrael and Eretz Yisrael
during the period between Yehoshua's conquest and the
Babylonian exile. Ramban will be our Rebbe in this journey of discovery.

Here is the Talmudic statement (Ta'anis 29a):

וכתיב, ותשא כל העדה ויתנו את קולם ויבכו העם בלילה ההוא. אמר
רבה אמר רבי יוחנן: אותה לילה ליל תשעה באב היה. אמר להם הקדוש
ברוך הוא: אתם בכיתם בכיה של חנם – ואני קובע לכם בכיה לדורות.
It is written, *The entire congregation broke out in wailing. The
people wept on that night* (BeMidbar 14:1). Rabbah taught
in the name of R. Yochanan: That night was Tish'ah
B'Av. God said to them: "On this night you cried for

32

5. The Episode of the Spies Revisited

no reason at all; I will make this into a night of tears throughout your exile."

It is not for nothing that the Beis HaMikdash was destroyed on Tish'ah B'Av, the very date upon which the spies wrought their ravages. Sforno's assertion seems to be confirmed.

The passage from Ramban that we are about to learn is so shattering in its implications that we will ease into it slowly. It matters a great deal that we get it right. First, though, we need to reconsider BeMidbar 14:31, a verse that we quoted in the previous chapter but only the first half of which we translated.

Here is the latter half of the verse.

... וטפכם אשר אמרתם לבז יהיה והבאתי אתם וידעו את הארץ אשר
מאסתם בה.

The first few words are simple enough: *As for your children, concerning whom you said, "They will be taken captive."* What is to happen to these children? If we translate literally, we have: *I will bring them [to the land] and they will "know" the land that you despised.* Taken thus, the verse contrasts the "children" to "you." *You* will never get to know the land, but your children will.

This translation is borne out by the parallel verse in Devarim 1:39:

וטפכם אשר אמרתם לבז יהיה ובניכם אשר לא ידעו היום טוב ורע
המה יבאו שמה ולהם אתננה והם יירשוה.
As for your children, concerning whom you said, "They will be taken captive," your sons who today are too young to differentiate between good and evil, THEY WILL COME THERE, TO THEM WILL I GIVE IT AND THEY WILL INHERIT IT.

I think we can all agree that this is what a simple read-

33

ing yields. However, we will see that Ramban has a very different perspective on the BeMidbar verse. Here is the passage by Ramban:

ואמרו רבותינו (תענית כט א) הם בכו בכיה של חנם ואני אקבע להם
בכיה לדורות. ולא ידעתי מאיזה רמז שבפרשה הוציאו זה. אבל מקרא
מלא הוא (תהלים קו כד–כז), וימאסו בארץ חמדה ולא האמינו לדברו
וירגנו באהליהם ולא שמעו בקול ה' וישא ידו להם להפיל אותם במדבר
ולהפיל זרעם בגוים ולזרותם בארצות. אולי ידרש זה מפסוק (לא)
וטפכם אשר אמרתם לבז יהיה, יאמר וטפכם כאשר אמרתם לבז יהיה
בבא עת פקודתם כי אני פוקד עון אבות על בנים, והבאתי אותם **עתה
שידעו את הארץ ידיעה בלבד, אבל לא שייירשו אותה לדורות.** והכתוב
ירמוז בכיוצא בזה, ולא ירצה לגזור רעה רק בענין תוכחת על תנאי.
Our Sages taught that *The Jews wept for no reason at all; I
[HaShem] will make this into a night of tears throughout their
exile.*" However, myself I cannot see how the Sages derived this lesson from the text of our *parashah*.

We do see this idea stated quite clearly in Tehillim:
*They despised the land which they should have loved . . . so
He swore to have them die in the desert, and to drive their
children out among the nations and to disperse them among the
lands.* [That given, we must assume some source in the
Chumash. Now what might this be?] Perhaps the Sages
translated the beginning of Devarim 1:39 as follows: *As
for your children, as you have said, they will be taken captive.*
However, this will not take place now, but much later
in history, when the time [of the Destruction] will have
come. . . .

[What, then, is the meaning of the second half of the
verse? It is this:] *I will bring them*—meaning, now—*so
that they shall get to know the land*—but only for the purpose of
"knowing" the land, and not to inherit it permanently.

This daring interpretation opens up whole vistas of
implications. But we will not be able to appreciate even
a fraction of these until we more closely analyze the episode of the spies. The rest of this book will be devoted

to that task. For the moment, however, we will limit ourselves to one very basic question: How can Ramban maintain that our entry into Eretz Yisrael was never meant to be permanent, that it was more in the nature of getting to know the place than actually moving in? How can this be the true interpretation, when it seems to be contradicted by the verse from Devarim that we cited above?

We will analyze the texts carefully and, in the end, reach a conclusion. First, though, we have the time for a little detour.

Here is a thought: our Seder night is structured around four mandatory cups of wine. The Yerushalmi offers a number of ideas with which these cups might be associated. Let us, for the purposes of this essay, assume that they parallel the well-known four expressions of redemption that occur in the *parashah* of VaEira (Shemos 6:6-8). Here is the passage where these are to be found:

ו. לכן אמר לבני ישראל אני יהוה **והוצאתי** אתכם מתחת סבלת מצרים **והצלתי** אתכם מעבדתם **וגאלתי** אתכם בזרוע נטויה ובשפטים גדלים.

ז. **ולקחתי** אתכם לי לעם והייתי לכם לאלהים וידעתם כי אני יהוה אלהיכם המוציא אתכם מתחת סבלות מצרים.

ח. **והבאתי אתכם** אל הארץ אשר נשאתי את ידי לתת אתה לאברהם ליצחק וליעקב ונתתי אתה לכם מורשה אני יהוה.

6. Therefore, say to the Children of Israel, "I am HaShem. *I shall take you out* from under the burdens of Egypt, *save you* from having to serve them and *redeem* you with an outstretched arm and with great wonders.

7. *I will take you* as a people....

8. *And I will bring you* to the land which I swore to give to Avraham, Yitzchak and Ya'akov, and I will give it to you as an inheritance. I am HaShem."

There is a great deal of conjecture concerning *and I will bring you* (verse 8). Why does that not qualify as a fifth expression of redemption? Should we not have five cups of wine? *Sefer HaManhig* suggests that *I will bring you* describes no action that was involved in the redemption; it is no more than a promise that the Israelites were to be taken to Eretz Yisrael. There are, however, Rishonim—Torah authorities who lived roughly between the eleventh and sixteenth centuries—who feel that *I will bring you* should also be considered an expression of redemption, and they believe that we do in fact have the option to drink a fifth cup of wine (cf. *Ba'aley Hatosafos* on Shemos 12:8).

It seems to me that Ramban might well agree that *I will bring you* is an expression of redemption. However, he would maintain that we do not celebrate this promise with a cup of wine for the simple reason that it was never fulfilled. Certainly, in the context in which it appears, this expression cannot be read as promising a "getting acquainted" visit. It surely implies that the Ribbono shel Olam will bring us to our home, and "home" is, of course, forever. Thus, no cup of wine would be appropriate for *I will bring you*, since it never happened.

That said, we must now concentrate on working out what might be Ramban's options in dealing with the verse from Devarim that we noted above. It certainly seems that *knowing* the land—as Ramban understands it—cannot coexist with *inheriting* the land.

Our short excursus on the phrase *I will bring you* can now stand us in good stead. Here is a chart which juxtaposes, and so enables us to compare, the three sources with which we are concerned.

5. The Episode of the Spies Revisited

DEVARIM	SHLACH	VAEIRA
וטפכם אשר אמרתם לבז יהיה ובניכם אשר לא ידעו היום טוב ורע המה יבאו שמה ולהם אתננה והם יירשוה.	וטפכם אשר אמרתם לבז יהיה (רמב"ן: כאשר אמרתם) והבאתי אתם וידעו את הארץ (רמב"ן: עתה שידעו את הארץ ידיעה בלבד, אבל לא שיירשו אותה).	והבאתי אתכם אל הארץ אשר נשאתי את ידי לתת אתה לאברהם ליצחק וליעקב ונתתי אתה לכם מורשה אני ידוד.
As for your children, concerning whom you said, "They will be taken captive," your sons who today are too young to differentiate between good and evil—they *will come* there. *To them I will give it, and they will inherit it.*	As for your children, concerning whom you said, "They will be taken captive" (Ramban: and your children, who will be, as you said, taken captive), *I will bring* them and they will "know" the land. (Ramban: Now they will only know the land, but not inherit it.)	*And I will bring* you to the land which I had sworn to give to Avraham, Yitzchak and Ya'akov, *and I will give it to you as an inheritance.* I am HaShem.

The chart above makes it clear that the Devarim wording conforms in most details to VaEira's promise. The Ribbono shel Olam will *give* them the land[2] and they will inherit it.[3]

How will Ramban deal with this?

The secret lies in the contrasting verbal forms used in the Shlach and Devarim passages.

Let us recall our conclusion above that *I will bring* in VaEira and Shlach implies permanency. The Ribbono shel Olam promised to bring us home for good.

Moreover, as Rashi teaches us at Devarim 1:8, this promise presaged a miraculous entry into the land. No weapons would be required, no wars would have to be fought.[4]

Now, Devarim purposely changes *I will* BRING into *they will* COME. At this stage, the Ribbono shel Olam is, as it were, out of the picture. The Jews will come to Eretz Yisrael by their own force of arms. That, of course, changes everything. Once this is established, the expressions *I will give it to them* and *they will inherit it*, although they are the same as the ones used in VaEira, take on an entirely different connotation. *I will give it to them* no longer means *I will bring them miraculously to their eternal home*, but *I will help them to victory*. And *they will inherit it* no longer means *they will take it over as an eternal heritage*, but *they will pass it on to their children as long as they remain in the country*.

In the Shlach passage, the word-phrase *I will bring* is maintained. Since *they will know the land* makes it clear that the conquest will not be a permanent one, there was no need to change the original language. It is clear that the meaning is that God will help in their battles and in that sense it can be said that *He will bring them to the land*.[5]

We have now seen that it is possible to accommodate both the Shlach and the Devarim passages to VaEira.[6] We will continue to study the import of Ramban's assertion in the coming chapters.

6.

The Spies
and the
Golden Calf

Here is a summary of what we have learned in the
last two chapters.

Shlomo HaMelech's Beis HaMikdash was,
from the beginning, doomed to destruction. At the very
moment that it was being built, the moment in which our
hold on Eretz Yisrael seemed finally to be consolidated,
when the last missing piece to complete the Jewish presence in the land was put in place, the specter of destruction and dispersal was a ghoul-like presence among the
celebrants. We do not know whether the people were
aware of the dimensions of the tragedy, but certainly
Shlomo HaMelech knew that this was not the Beis
HaMikdash that the Ribbono shel Olam wanted. Theirs
was not the Jewish presence in the land towards which
the Ribbono shel Olam had steered history.

It is true that, given the realities, the inauguration was a
matter for great rejoicing. But only because things were
as they had become. It was not, it could not be, the real
thing.

The spies were at fault. After that debacle, nothing
was ever again the same.

The time has come to think about this sad story more deeply.

Both the sin of the golden calf and the sin of the spies wrought major dislocations in Jewish destiny. The former left us with a lesser Torah,[1] the latter with an impaired relationship to the Ribbono shel Olam. Without attempting any groundbreaking analysis of these two calamities[2] at this point, we will note some differences between the marks each of them left upon Jewish history. Our discoveries will help us put the sin of the spies into sharper relief.

There are at least three issues that should help us along the way. We will take them one by one.

I. ON THE DAY THAT I MAKE AN ACCOUNTING[3]

The golden calf remains with us in a way that the spies do not. To understand the implications, we will examine Shemos 32:34: *Now lead the people to where I have told you.... [However,] on the day that I make an accounting, I shall reckon their sin against them.*[4]

What does the second phrase mean and how does it connect to the earlier part of the verse?

Here are Ramban's comments:

ועתה לך נחה את העם. כי אחרי שנחמתי מכלותם נחם אתה אל אשר דברתי לך, אל מקום הכנעני והאמורי וגו', אבל לא רצה להזכיר כן שזה דרך כעס, כאומר מה שדברתי לך אעשה לכבודך, אבל לא אשא חטאתם, כי ביום פקדי ופקדתי עליהם חטאתם, אפקוד אותו עליהם אחרי בואם אל הארץ, וזה רמז לעת שיגלו ממנה, או למה שאמרו רבותינו (סנהדרין קב.) שאין לך פורענות שאין בה אוקיא מעון העגל.

"Now lead the people to where I have told you." This, of course, refers to the land of the Canaanites and the Emorites. Still, the Ribbono shel Olam did not identify these places by name, because He was speaking in anger.

The sense is as follows: "Since I told you to take the Jews to this place, I will—out of respect for you[5]—allow

40

6. The Spies and the Golden Calf

this plan to continue. However, I have not forgiven their sin,[6] and therefore I will still punish them. This will take place only after they have come to the land." This hints at the fact that one day they will be exiled, or it may be connected to the Talmudic comment that any punishment that the Jewish people will ever have to endure will have mixed into it some residual suffering from the sin of the golden calf.

Ramban makes it very clear that the sin of the golden calf was not forgiven in any real sense,[7] and that therefore punishment would be meted out over the centuries.

It seems justifiable to ask why nothing similar was put in place for the sin of the spies. Why is there no account-taking in that case?

I think that the answer is simple: The sin of the golden calf had a beginning and an end. When it was all over, Moshe Rabbeinu threw himself into prayer on behalf of Klal Yisrael, and succeeded spectacularly. He elicited God's forgiveness in the form of the revelation of the Thirteen Traits of Compassion. A new set of Tablets, the tablets of the Ten Commandments, was given, albeit under different conditions and at a lesser level of sanctity than the original ones. The Ribbono shel Olam Himself permitted the trek to Eretz Yisrael to continue as originally planned. This was no longer in the merit of Moshe Rabbeinu, but because God's own purpose had been restored. The story is finished. There is, however, one piece of unfinished business, and that is the punishment for a very heinous sin. This will be exacted *on the day that I make an accounting.*

The episode of the spies is in no way comparable. The appalling upheaval that it generated within Klal Yisrael never underwent a closure comparable to the giving of the second Tablets. The Ribbono shel Olam never really forgave the sin,[8] nor did Moshe Rabbeinu pray for its total obliteration as he had done on the earlier occasion. (For all this, see chart on page 43-45.) That being so, there was no need for a provision that would allow a fraction of the punishment to be added to other tragedies that would occur in the future, because these same tragedies would themselves be the direct outcome of the episode of the spies.

It is true that the sin of the spies never resulted in the awful threat of a *day that I make an accounting.* That is not because it was any less terrible than the sin of the golden calf, but because, at least in terms of its aftermath, it was infinitely worse.

2. THE PRAYERS OF MOSHE RABBEINU

Even a cursory glance at BeMidbar 14:18 (Parshas Shlach) makes it clear that the Traits of Compassion that Moshe Rabbeinu chose to invoke in his prayers during the episode of the spies are not completely congruent to the Thirteen Traits of Compassion that we know so well from his prayers in Parashas Ki Sissa. On the facing page is a chart that will make this clear. I will provide Ramban's explanation—where available—of the various omissions in the blanks left in the Shlach column.

6. The Spies and the Golden Calf

כי תשא	שלח
ה'	ה'
ה'	
אל	
רחום וחנון	ולא ידעתי למה לא הזכיר "רחום וחנון" אולי ידע משה כי הדין מתוח עליהם ולא ימחול לעולם. לכן לא ביקש רק אריכת אפים, שלא ימיתם כאיש אחד. ובעבור שלא בקש עתה אלא אריכת אפים, אמר לו "סלחתי כדבריך" שאהיה להם ארך אפים ורב חסד.
ארך אפים ורב חסד	ארך אפים ורב חסד
ואמת	כי במדת האמת יהיו חייבים
נוצר חסד לאלפים	כי לא בזכות אבות נתפלל משה עכשיו, ולא הזכיר בתפלתו הזאת לאברהם ליצחק וליעקב כלל. והטעם בעבור שהארץ נתנה לאבות ומהם ירשוה, והם מורדים באבותם ולא היו חפצים במתנה שלהם, אשר האבות היו בוחרים בה מאד, והיאך יאמר "אשר נשבעת בהם בך וכל הארץ הזאת אתן לזרעכם" והם אומרים אי אפשנו במתנה זו?
נושא עון ופשע	נושא עון ופשע
וחטאה	ולא הזכיר "חטאה" בעבור שאלה מזידים ופושעים
ונקה (לא ינקה)	ונקה (לא ינקה)

43

KI SISSA	SHLACH
HaShem	HaShem
HaShem	
God	
Merciful and gracious	I do not know why the verse does not say *merciful and gracious*. Perhaps Moshe knew that judgment was hanging over their heads and that God would not forgive them. Therefore, he only requested *slow to anger*, so that HaShem would not wipe them out in one blow. And since now he only asked for *slow to anger*, God told him, *I have forgiven as you have spoken*—meaning, *I will indeed be slow to anger.*
Slow to anger and filled with lovingkindness	Slow to anger and filled with lovingkindness
And true.	Because judged by the trait of *truth*, they would be guilty.
Creating lovingkindness for thousands	For at this point, Moshe did not invoke the merit of the patriarchs; in his prayer he made no mention at all of Avraham, Yitzchak and Ya'akov. The reason is that the land was given to the patriarchs, but although the Jews inherited it from them, they rebelled against their forefathers and rejected their gift, one that the patriarchs had so greatly cherished. So how could

6. The Spies and the Golden Calf

	Moshe pray and remind God, "You promised the patriarchs that *all this land I will give to your offspring*," when the Jews are now saying that they don't want this gift?
Forgiving sin and iniquity	Forgiving sin and iniquity.
And transgression	Moshe made no mention of *transgression*, since they were rebellious and iniquitous.
And as for erasing, (He will surely not erase)....	And as for erasing, (He will surely not erase)....

Ramban's remarks explaining the absence of any mention of *merciful and gracious* are of particular significance. Ramban says quite clearly that the Ribbono shel Olam will *never* forgive the sin of the spies.

Only with this point well understood can we approach Ramban on 14:19. There he notes that when Moshe Rabbeinu told the story of the spies shortly before his death (as reported in Devarim 1:22 and onwards), he made no mention of the fact that he had prayed on the people's behalf. This, in contrast to his account of the sin of the golden calf, in which his prayers figure prominently. Here is what Ramban says:

ולא הזכיר להם במרגלים שהתפלל עליהם כלל. וכל זה מן הטעם שהזכרתי, כי הוא לא התפלל למחול להם אלא שישא להם ויאריך אפו ויפקוד עון אבות על בנים, ולא היתה תפלתו שלימה עליהם, ועל כן לא הזכירה להם כי היו יכולין לטעון עליו.

He did not mention that he had prayed for them ... because he never asked the Ribbono shel Olam for complete forgiveness, only that He should show patience and not allow His anger free rein all at once.

45

Moshe Rabbeinu failed to mention his prayer because it surely fell far short of what the people would have wanted. He feared that they would feel a sense of betrayal.

Ramban's structural model of what occurred works perfectly once the base upon which he erects it is granted. It was a time in which the faculty of justice held sway.

Why was it so? Where, at this time when it was so desperately needed, was the mercy of our Compassionate Father?

Then there is another point. Ramban explains the omission of *creating lovingkindness for thousands* because this phrase seeks to invoke the merit of the patriarchs. Under the circumstances, this was inappropriate. Eretz Yisrael was so central to each one of the patriarchs that their descendants, willing as they were to give up on the land so readily, had no right to demand the patriarchs' intercession. Even now these descendants were rebelling against what had been most precious to the patriarchs.

Well and good. But was the absolute rejection of idol worship also not central to the lives of the patriarchs? Why, when some among Klal Yisrael served the golden calf, was this not a sign that they had become alienated from the values that animated the lives of their forefathers? Was not, then, the episode of the golden calf likewise a rebellion against all that the patriarchs had held dear?

A very similar question might be asked about Ramban's explanation for the omission of *transgression*. Ramban maintains that since *transgression* connotes inadvertent transgression, it is inappropriate in the episode of the spies, because the Jews' sin was committed with full knowledge and, indeed, with rebellious intent. But was not the episode of the golden calf also instigated by people who knew full well that what they were doing was absolutely forbidden? Why, if *transgression* was appropriate in the episode of the golden calf, can it not be used for the spies?

From all these points, it seems clear that there was something extremely pernicious about the sin of the spies that puts it into a category of its own. We will need to find out what it was.[9]

3. AS YOU HAVE SPOKEN

In the episode of the spies, Moshe Rabbeinu ends his prayer with the words *I beg You to forgive the sin that these people have committed, as befits Your great kindness.* Then we are told: *HaShem said, "I have forgiven as you have spoken."*[10]

Ramban clearly takes *as you have spoken* as having a restrictive function. We recall from what we have learned in the previous section that Moshe Rabbeinu's prayers in this matter were less than ambitious. He did not ask that God grant total absolution, only that the punishment be spread over the generations. After Ramban makes this point, he continues, "And since now he only asked for *length of days*, God told him, *I have forgiven as you have spoken.* I can accede to your prayer just because it is so limited in scope."

Rashi appears to be even more restrictive than is Ramban. On *I have forgiven as you have spoken,* he writes: *in acceptance of your argument that if I were to destroy Klal Yisrael the gentile nations would misinterpret this as a sign of weakness.* The implication is that Moshe Rabbeinu's prayer was completely ignored. Only his argument based upon the need to avoid a desecration of God's Name elicited a response.[11]

Clearly the sin of the spies penetrated very deeply into the Jewish soul. It will be our task in the coming chapters to examine why.

7.

Heresy

H ere is something to think about.
The phrase *I believe with perfect faith* is no
stranger to us. The grand structure of Judaism
rises upon a stratum of axioms, which, if we take the word
emunah—faith—in its most literal sense (from *omon—
to nurture, to be a wet nurse*), can be said to sustain and
lend coherence to our *emunah*. We are a nation of believers.

Rambam in Hilchos Teshuvah, Chapter 3, deals with
the issue of heresy. He outlines a hierarchy of heretics
and false believers, a hierarchy consisting of five levels,
beginning with the complete nonbeliever—as follows:

חמשה הן הנקראים מינים: האומר שאין שם אלוה ואין לעולם מנהיג,
והאומר שיש שם מנהיג אבל הן שנים או יותר, והאומר שיש שם רבון
אחד אבל שהוא גוף ובעל תמונה, וכן האומר שאינו לבדו הראשון וצור
לכל, וכן העובד כוכב או מזל וזולתו כדי להיות מליץ בינו ובין רבון
העולמים כל אחד מחמשה אלו הוא מין.

There are five categories [of heretics]:

1. One who maintains that there is no God and that the
world is left to happenstance.

7. Heresy

2. One who maintains that there is a deity but believes it to consist of two or more.

3. One who maintains that there is a unique deity but that it is corporeal.

4. One who maintains that this deity is not alone in being the first and the creator of everything.

5. Someone who worships a star or a *mazal* or anything similar, in order that it should act as an intermediary between him and the Ribbono shel Olam.

Each one of these is a *min*.

It is easy to see that the first four in this list deal with the character of the Ribbono shel Olam, whereas the fifth concerns the relationship between man and God. But why does this last category appear in the same list with the other four?

The conclusion seems inescapable. There must be a common factor. It is this: If any of the first four beliefs is maintained, the *Ribbono shel Olam* is (so to speak) diminished; whereas if the fifth is accepted, *man* is diminished. And it is as heinous a heresy to doubt man's grandeur as it is to doubt God's. It is no small matter that we have unmediated access to the Ribbono shel Olam. Deny that and what do you have? A parody of the *image of God*, a poor specimen whom the Ribbono shel Olam will not tolerate in His Presence.

What does all this have to do with the spies? The episode of the spies is the story of a people who were unable to believe in themselves. They were not heretics in the formal sense of the word, but they were afflicted by the same corrosive self-doubt that underlies the fifth category. They gave no credence to the greatness which, had they but believed it, lay within their grasp.

Let us take a look at two verses in Devarim, Chapter 1, and open our hearts to feel the sorrow and the pain of a missed moment, of great opportunities squandered.

Here is the first one that we will consider.

כב. וַתִּקְרְבוּן אֵלַי כֻּלְּכֶם וַתֹּאמְרוּ נִשְׁלְחָה אֲנָשִׁים לְפָנֵינוּ וְיַחְפְּרוּ לָנוּ אֶת הָאָרֶץ וְיָשִׁבוּ אֹתָנוּ דָּבָר אֶת הַדֶּרֶךְ אֲשֶׁר נַעֲלֶה בָּהּ וְאֵת הֶעָרִים אֲשֶׁר נָבֹא אֲלֵיהֶן.

22. All of you banded together against me [Moshe Rabbeinu], saying, "Let us send men ahead of us so that they may spy out the land for us, and let them bring back information by which route we should go up against it and which are the cities against which we will come."

It is the end of the fortieth year. Moshe Rabbeinu, recognizing that the time has come to make his farewells, embarks upon a series of hortatory speeches. Understandably, the episode of the spies is uppermost in his mind. As he will say in verse 37 and as we have discussed in previous essays, it is that debacle that sealed his own fate. *He* would not enter Eretz Yisrael because *they* had failed to appreciate its worth. He felt the need to spell out what had gone so terribly wrong.

Here is the Rashi on this verse.

VERSE	RASHI
וַתִּקְרְבוּן אֵלַי כֻּלְּכֶם All of you banded together against me	בערבוביא, ולהלן הוא אומר (דברים ה, כ–כא) ותקרבון אלי כל ראשי שבטיכם וזקניכם ותאמרו הן הראנו וגו', אותה קריבה היתה הוגנת. ילדים מכבדים את הזקנים ושלחום לפניהם, וזקנים מכבדים את הראשים ללכת לפניהם, אבל כאן, ותקרבון אלי כולכם, בערבוביא. ילדים דוחפין את הזקנים וזקנים דוחפין את הראשים. *All of you* implies that they came in undisciplined disarray.

50

7. Heresy

This, in contrast to Devarim 5:20–21, where the wording is, *Then the leaders of your tribes and the elders approached me, saying* .... On that occasion, all was done in an appropriate manner: the youngsters deferred to the elders, the elders to the leaders. Here, however, there was no order at all. Youngsters jostled elders, elders jostled leaders.

ותאמרו נשלחה אנשים לפנינו ויחפרו לנו את הארץ Saying, "Let us send men ahead of us so that they may spy out the land for us,	
וישבו אתנו דבר And let them bring back information	באיזה לשון הם מדברים. What language they speak.
את הדרך אשר נעלה בה By which route we should go up against it	אין דרך שאין בה עקמימות. Every road has its complications.
ואת הערים אשר נבא אליהן and which are the cities against which we will come."	תחלה לכבוש. Which cities we will first encounter in order to conquer.

At first reading, the people's concerns sound sensible and prudent; one generally does not go into battle without adequate intelligence. Still, not all is well. The unseemly way in which they approached Moshe Rabbeinu showed that there was panic in the air, and panic is a surefire indication of serious inner malaise.

What had gone wrong? For an answer, let us consider the verse immediately preceding the one we are discussing. Let us remember that it is Moshe Rabbeinu speaking. In that preceding verse he says:

ראה נתן ידוד אלהיך לפניך את הארץ **עלה רש** כאשר דבר ידוד אלהי אבתיך לך אל תירא ואל תחת.

See, HaShem your God has set out the land before you. *Go up and possess it,* just as HaShem the God of your fathers promised you. You have nothing to fear, nothing to make you hesitate (Devarim 1:21).

We have italicized *Go up and possess it.* These are the words that hold the key to the solution of our problem. They refer back to verse 8, where the Ribbono shel Olam had said, *See, I have set out the land before you.* COME AND POSSESS THE LAND *that Hashem promised your forefathers, Avraham, Yitzchak and Ya'akov, to give to them and their offspring after them.* On the phrase *Come and possess it,* Rashi remarks that Moshe is telling his people, "*Nobody will try to stop you. There is no need for you to make war.*" And Rashi adds, *Had they not sent the spies, they would not have had any need for weapons.*[1]

Taken together with the verse immediately following (*All of you banded together*), the implications are shattering. Moshe Rabbeinu is inviting Klal Yisrael to soar above the ordinary. They can walk into the land unopposed. They will, if they can bring themselves to rise to the challenge, be invincible. The Canaanite hordes will melt away before them as the sea had fled at their approach just a short year earlier. That is the promise which Moshe Rabbeinu held out to them.

And they? It is as though they had not heard a word. Moshe Rabbeinu had been talking about a people cradled in God's arms, such that no human force could stand up against them, and they, instead of hurling themselves into that embrace, are busy thinking strategy. What language? Which road? What city needs to be conquered first? It is as if they had heard nothing. They could not picture themselves rising on eagles' wings. They knew only how to plod along like everybody else, clay feet firmly on the ground. They hoped they might be stronger than the Canaanites, but the idea did not penetrate to them that they might be different. God spoke poetry, they heard prose.

Earlier in this essay, we remarked that the tragedy of the spies was that the people did not believe in themselves. We now have a better idea of what this might mean. We will continue to explore this concept in the next chapter.

8.

An Introduction to Our Analysis of Parashas HaMeraglim

H ere is some background information which will ease our way as we get deeper and deeper into our analysis of Parashas HaMeraglim. Some of the points we will raise here will not be news to most of our readers; others are less well known. I have the feeling that everybody will be happy to have the information provided in an organized manner, ready to be consulted as the need arises.

1. The story of the spies appears twice in the Torah; once as part of the BeMidbar narrative in Parashas Shlach, the other as part of Moshe Rabbeinu's farewell address in Devarim. But there are significant differences, and we are left with the task of cutting and pasting, creating a seamless whole from two very different parts. At the end of this chapter, I will provide quotes which will make it a little easier to grasp the issues involved.

2. There is a wide-ranging disagreement between Rashi and Ramban concerning the propriety of the people's request (in the Devarim passage) that spies

should be sent. Throughout his commentary, Rashi faults the people for asking. God had told them that the land was good, and they should have realized that there was no need for further inquiries.

Ramban, while admitting that Rashi's ideas are reflected in Chazal, nevertheless maintains that the request was reasonable and is therefore defensible: Things began to go wrong only when the spies came back and delivered their negative and frightening report.

Nevertheless, after working out his argument in great detail, Ramban comes at least partway back to the position of Rashi and Chazal: Perhaps, given all the miracles which the people had experienced, they should have trusted God more and worried less.

3. The passage in Shlach begins with the words *Shlach lecha* (שלח לך), whose literal translation is *send for yourself*. This literal rendering is just how Rashi takes the phrase and, as he reads it, it means, *I leave it up to you. If you want to, you may permit the people to send the spies, but this does not accord with My wishes.*

Ramban, for his part, leaves the word *lechah* (לך) untranslated, deeming it a purely idiomatic usage in this context.[1] *Shlach lecha* is to be rendered simply, as *Send!*

This leaves the deck clear for Ramban's first interpretation—that is, for his view that there was no opprobrium of any kind attached to sending the Meraglim. The Ribbono shel Olam could have simply allowed the story to develop as it is described in the Devarim account. The people ask to send spies, Moshe Rabbeinu agrees and, forthwith, chooses a representative from each tribe to be a part of the expedition. However, God wants to give the enterprise the imprimatur of a Divine command, thus making it more likely that it will meet with the kind of success which it deserves. He therefore commands Moshe Rabbeinu to send spies (the BeMidbar passage) without reference to the fact that the people had, on their own, already broached this idea.

Even in Ramban's subsequent partial about-face, his willingness to concede that, given the many miraculous salvations which the Jews had experienced, they should not have requested that spies be sent, he still maintains that the Shlach! *Send!* of BeMidbar is an absolute command (in contradistinction to Rashi, who sees it as not a command but a grudging permission). Ramban compares this to another instance in Jewish history where a realistic appraisal of what could reasonably be expected of the people as they then were, convinced God to issue a command which, had circumstances hewed more closely to the ideal, would not have been necessary: the sad story told in I Shmuel 8:4.

There we learn how the people came to Shmuel towards the end of his life and demanded that he appoint a king over them. The story is a complex one, and an analysis would take us much too far away from our present subject. Suffice it to say that the request was ill conceived and, under the circumstances, should not have been made. Shmuel, horrified at the people's demand, turned to God in prayer. God answered that he should do what the people asked. He should not consider their request as a rejection of his own leadership. It was, rather, a rejection of the Ribbono shel Olam Himself.

Ramban makes the comparison between the two situations but does not say in so many words what principle is at work. My sense is, and for this I found confirmation in the Sha'arey Aharon, in his glosses on Shlach, that he is affirming that God leads us in the directions in which we, ourselves, choose to go.[2] Once the people asked for a king, once the people insisted that they wanted to send spies, a new reality was created. People with so little appreciation for what Shmuel was able to give them did indeed require a king. People who dared not trust them-

8. Our Analysis of Parshas HaMeraglim

selves to God's direct stewardship would be served best
by having spies find out what they could about the land
they were about to enter.

HaRav Ya'akov Kamenetzky, in his *Iyyunim BaMikra*,
seems to agree with this second interpretation of the
Ramban. Although he does not mention the Ramban, he
too believes that once the people had made their choice
that spies should be sent—wrong-headed though it
was—it became necessary to indulge them. He bases
his assumption on BeMidbar 13:3, *So Moshe sent them*
[the spies] *from the wilderness of Paran*, BY THE MOUTH
OF HASHEM.... The expression *by the mouth of HaShem*
normally denotes a message from the Urim VeTumim.
Clearly if we postulate (as our Sages do) that the request
for the spies was inappropriate, there must have been a
change of heart.

For the remaining chapters in this book, we will follow
Rav Kamenetzky's precedent and approach the story of
the spies as one of a precipitous fall in the spiritual standing of the people. The reverberations which left their
dreadful marks all over our history, as we have demonstrated previously, are all traceable to that tragic but in-
controvertible fact. At this one all-important moment,
we failed. And nothing afterwards could ever again be
the same.

Here are the quotes which I promised at the beginning
of this essay. In Devarim we read:

כב. ותקרבון אלי כלכם ותאמרו נשלחה אנשים לפנינו ויחפרו לנו את
הארץ וישבו אתנו דבר את הדרך אשר נעלה בה ואת הערים אשר נבא
אליהן.

כג. וייטב בעיני הדבר ואקח מכם שנים עשר אנשים. . . .

22. All of you banded together against me, saying,
"Let us send men ahead of us so that they may spy out

the land for us, and let them bring back information by which route we should go up against it and which are the cities against which we will come.

23. And the matter appeared good in my eyes, and I took twelve men from among you....

We conclude with the verses of Shlach (BeMidbar 13:1-3):

א. וידבר ידוד אל משה לאמר.

ב. שלח לך אנשים ויתרו את ארץ כנען אשר אני נתן לבני ישראל איש אחד איש אחד למטה אבתיו תשלחו כל נשיא בהם.

ג. וישלח אתם משה ממדבר פארן על פי ידוד כלם אנשים ראשי בני ישראל המה.

1. And HaShem spoke to Moshe, saying:

2. Send forth for yourself men to spy out the land of Canaan that I am giving to the Children of Israel—one man for each tribe, each man a prince of his tribe.

3. And Moshe sent them forth from the Wilderness of Paran by the mouth of HaShem, all of them men who were the heads of the Children of Israel.

9.

Moments That Move Our History

What happened? What did we do to ourselves? What became of the promise that had been so rich? One slip and history weeps. Think of the Babylonian hordes. Think of the Roman centurions. Think of the Crusaders. Think West; think East. Think of the gas and the smoke, the lash and the tearing dogs. Think of the Siberian wastes, the atrophied minds, the starving millions; the fear, the dreadful fear. None of it should have been. None of it need have been. We have only ourselves to blame. How could it have happened?

Let us go back to the beginnings.

In the last chapter, we saw that the episode of the spies is told twice: once as part of the BeMidbar narrative in Shlach and then as part of Moshe Rabbeinu's farewell address in Devarim. The two stories are not the same, and we are left with the task of cutting and pasting, creating a seamless whole from two very different parts.

If we can do this, it will help, but it will not be enough. We will still not know why the Torah would want to tell us one complex story by splitting it into two simple ones. Why does Shlach tell nothing of how the people had earlier come to importune Moshe Rabbeinu, and why does Moshe Rabbeinu mention nothing of God's command to send the spies?

Let us take first things first. What actually happened, and in what sequence did things occur?

Here is the chronology as it appears to me. At each stage I will add a few lines that will make my reasoning clear. In order to get this done without undue repetition, I will be pulling together bits and pieces from earlier essays.

1. THE PEOPLE COME TO IMPORTUNE MOSHE RABBEINU. This is the beginning of the story. However, as we worked out in Chapter 7, the juxtaposition of this account with the earlier verse creates a dramatic background. The people want the spies not as a prudent preparation for a necessary war but as a rejection of God's offer to hand them the land miraculously, without any fighting. Our Sages detect an inexcusable panic, which is expressed in the unseemly manner in which the approach was made. Tragedy is in the making.

2. MOSHE RABBEINU ACQUIESCES TO THE REQUEST. He realizes that these are no longer the same people who only recently had stood at Sinai and reached for the heavens. They have changed. They refuse to be challenged; they want only that which is normal and, presumably, comfortable. They have rejected God's offer of a miraculous entry into the land. They are what they are and do not wish to be moved.

3. THE RIBBONO SHEL OLAM COMMANDS MOSHE RABBEINU TO SEND THE SPIES. This is the turning point of Jewish history. What has hitherto been a misguided grasping at straws driven by panic now becomes a divine command. Something ominous has happened. It is to the analysis of this sea change that I devote this essay.

9. Moments That Move Our History

What happened? Without Devarim's *all of you banded together against me*, there would have been no spies. Moreover, it is a terrible idea. Yet all of a sudden it becomes a mitzvah to send them. Why?[1]

We must begin with a passage from Ramban on VaYikra 26:11.[2] Ramban describes in detail how, in an ideal world, there would be no place for doctors. Health would be a gift to the righteous, sickness a scourge for the wicked. Maladies would succumb to repentance, not to medicines. Here is what he says:

אבל הדורש השם בנביא לא ידרוש ברופאים . . . והוא מאמרם שאין
דרכם של בני אדם ברפואות אלא שנהגו, אילו לא היה דרכם ברפואות
יחלה האדם כפי אשר יהיה עליו עונש חטאו ויתרפא ברצון ה', אבל הם
נהגו ברפואות והשם הניחם למקרי הטבעים.

Whenever sickness struck, people would go to the prophets for guidance. In such a society there would be no room for medical intervention. Cures would follow God's acceptance of the stricken person's repentance. Our Sages teach (Berachos 60a) that there is no natural need to resort to medicine in order to cure an illness; it is only that people have slipped into the habit of seeking it out. If people had not chosen to go to doctors, sickness would come about only as a divine punishment and would be cured without medication through the good will of the Ribbono shel Olam. However, mankind chose to walk the path of medical intervention, and as a result *God forsook them to the exigencies of nature.*

Man can live under the direct stewardship of the Ribbono shel Olam, or he can decide to go his own way. He and only he must decide. God does not impose Himself upon us. He is available to us should we want Him, He will recede within Himself if we prefer to go it alone. The final few words in this passage are ominous. We can distance ourselves from the Ribbono shel Olam to the extent that He leaves us to whatever nature has in store for us.

This is what happened when, so long ago, we allowed our attachment to bland, impersonal nature to blind our souls. There was really no need to worry about sending spies. God did not need them and, if all had gone as it should, we would have entered the land as honored guests. It is we who decided that this was not the path we wished to follow. The moment we demanded spies, it was clear that we had decided to prefer the exigencies of predictable nature to the unknowns of direct providence; that we had opted for independence, with all the horrors which this would entail, over submission.

Spies became a necessity.

God, as it were, sighed and commanded Moshe Rabbeinu to send spies.

There are indeed two stories. The first speaks of falling giants, the second of plodding dwarfs. The first is told by Moshe Rabbeinu as part of the strictures that were his parting gift to his failing students. "With you," he tells them, "an epoch died." The second is a straightforward account of history as it happened to a diminished people. BeMidbar is concerned not with what might have been but with what was.

This, to a large extent, is the sad story of the spies. Instead of walking into Eretz Yisrael as owners, we entered as conquerors. And that made all the difference.

We will conclude this chapter by explaining this last paragraph. In the next chapter, we will move on to the next stage of our explorations.

First, then, our assertion that had we chosen to trust the Ribbono shel Olam, we could have entered Eretz Yisrael as owners. To flesh out this bald statement, we go to Ramban on BeReishis 9:26. No'ach had punished his son Cham (who had abused him so shamefully) by condemning Cham's son, Canaan, to eternal slavery. Canaan was to be indentured to both Shem and Yeffes. Ramban explains the nature of his servitude to Shem. He writes:

והנה העביד כנען לשם . . . , רמז כי הוא ינחל ארצו וכל אשר לו, כי מה
שקנה עבד קנה רבו (פסחים פח:).
ונכתבה זאת הפרשה להודיע כי בחטאו היה כנען עבד עולם וזכה
אברהם בארצו.

No'ach's decree that Canaan was to be enslaved to Shem indicated that in the future Shem's descendants would take over Canaan's land and all that Canaan possessed. Shem would be justified in doing this because of the rule that whatever a slave owns really belongs to his owner.

Thus we can say that the Torah's purpose in telling the story of No'ach's drunken disgrace was to clear the way for Avraham's descendants to be legally entitled to the land that they would eventually take over.

The Ribbono shel Olam's disposition that the land which He intended to give to His children should first fall to the descendants of Canaan was motivated by Canaan's status as slave to Shem. In this way Canaan would build up the land, till its fields and build its cities, in order that Avraham's children would find their possessions ready and developed for them when the time would come for them to take possession.[3]

This truth underlies the Ribbono shel Olam's promise that no weapons would be required for the Israelites to enter the land. Since they were the rightful owners, there was no historical imperative that would make a war necessary. However, when Klal Yisrael refused to enter the land on those terms, when they insisted on sending spies in order to be able to take possession by force of arms, this entire plan lay in shambles. If they were going to base their claim to the land on the force of conquest, then their fate would be that of conquerors. They would have the land only as long as they were strong enough to hold on to it.

This is articulated by Rambam, Hilchos Beis HaBechirah 6:16. The context is as follows: There is a halachic question as to whether in the period between the destruction of the first Beis HaMikdash and the building of the second the agricultural laws that apply when the land is hallowed by Jewish possession continued to be binding. Did the "Jewish" status of the land that began with Yehoshua's conquest (the *kedushah rishonah*, "first sanctification") continue or not?

Rambam writes as follows:

. . . קדושת שאר א"י לעניין שביעית ומעשרות וכיוצא בהן לא קדשה לעתיד לבוא [כי] חיוב הארץ בשביעית ובמעשרות אינו אלא מפני שהוא כבוש רבים וכיון שנלקחה הארץ מידיהם בטל הכבוש ונפטרה מן התורה ממעשרות ומשביעית שהרי אינה מן ארץ ישראל.

The sanctity of the land relative to its agricultural laws does not carry over to the period following the destruction of the Beis HaMikdash. This is because it went into effect under the banner of "conquest," and therefore, once the land was taken away from the Jews, that "conquest" was no longer in effect and had no legal status.

Had they entered as owners, even a subsequent conquest would have left the sanctity of the land intact. However, since they were only conquerers the sanctity was lost the moment they themselves suffered defeat.

Let us now turn to some more explorations of the episode of the spies.

10.

Rejection

on a Large Scale

We have spent the last few essays exploring the people's tragic inability to make a really big-hearted gesture of surrender to God's willing embrace. In plumbing the distance of that dreadful freefall into small-minded self-assertion, we have almost forgotten that there was a second, perhaps more tragic,[1] chapter to this story. The people's failure did not end with their decision to go it alone. That was just the beginning. They not only insisted on sending the spies, but they then fell prey to the slander that the spies spread about the land. They were willing to give up on the whole venture upon which they had embarked with so much hope a few short months earlier. *Let us appoint a leader and return to Egypt.* Things do not get much worse than that.

Here is a question. What, if any, is the relationship between the two great failings that make up the depressing story of the spies? Are we able to—indeed, ought we—trace the second to the first, or are the two independent of one another? Would we have become so demoralized by the spies' report if we had not initially erred so dreadfully in wanting to send them? It is important that we understand what happened.

To begin with, what did the people mean when they said, *Let us appoint a leader and return to Egypt?*

There are two traditions, spread throughout Aggadic literature. The first equates this *leader* with idolatry.[2]

65

The people proposed to Moshe Rabbeinu that they put an idol at their head and that this idol should then lead them back to Egypt.

The second tradition seems even stranger. The people proposed to remove Moshe Rabbeinu and Aharon and to seek different leadership, men who would be willing to bring them back to Mitzrayim. The plan was to appoint Dasan and Aviram—the two men who, from the very beginning, had constantly sought to undermine Moshe and Aharon's authority.

Here is how Maharal (*Gevuros HaShem*) explains the relationship between Moshe Rabbeinu and Aharon on the one hand and Dasan and Aviram on the other:

כי כאשר זכו ישראל לשני אנשים נבדלים מכלל ישראל במעלה, והם משה ואהרן, גם זה לעמת זה, כי הרע הוא לעמת הטוב תמיד. לכך הם מישראל שני אנשים רשעים נבדלים לרע מתנגדים תמיד אל משה ותורתו, ולפיכך היו תמיד אלו השנים מתנגדים להם בעצמם. ובמדרש תהילים (ק"ו) בקשו ישראל במדבר למנות דתן במקומו של משה ואבירם במקומו של אהרן, שנאמר, נתנה ראש ונשובה מצרימה. ומה גרם לעכבכם? תפתח ארץ ותבלע דתן ותכס על עדת אבירם.

The divine law that requires balance between good and evil demanded that Moshe and Aharon, men whose spiritual stature made them unique, be balanced by two men, Dasan and Aviram, whose propensity for evil was altogether beyond that of anybody else in Israel.

Both alternatives are horrendous in their implications. The fact that such suggestions could have been made in all seriousness puts the episode of the spies on a plane all its own. None of the other sins that we committed in the wilderness can approach this one in the sheer nihilism that fired this rebellion.[3]

It will be useful to compare the three places in which the Jews looked back longingly to their servitude in Egypt.

10. Rejection on a Large Scale

	I.
SHEMOS 14 AT THE SEA OF REEDS	יב. הלא זה הדבר אשר דברנו אליך במצרים לאמר חדל ממנו ונעבדה את מצרים כי טוב לנו עבד את מצרים ממתנו במדבר. 12. "Is this not exactly what we had said to you in Egypt: 'Leave us alone and let us serve in Egypt, *because it is better that we serve in Egypt* than die in the desert.'"
BEMIDBAR 11 GRUMBLING ABOUT THE MANNA	ד. והאספסף אשר בקרבו התאוו תאוה. . . . יח. ואל העם תאמר התקדשו למחר ואכלתם בשר כי בכיתם באזני ידוד לאמר מי יאכלנו בשר כי טוב לנו במצרים ונתן ידוד לכם בשר ואכלתם. 4. And the mixed multitude in their midst conceived a great longing. . . . 18. "And tell the people: Prepare yourself for tomorrow, when you shall eat meat, for you wept in the ears of HaShem, saying, 'Who will feed us meat, *for it was good for us in Egypt.*' And HaShem will give you meat, and you will eat."
BEMIDBAR 14 THE SPIES	א. ותשא כל העדה ויתנו את קולם ויבכו העם בלילה ההוא. ב. וילנו על משה ועל אהרן כל בני ישראל ויאמרו אלהם כל העדה לו מתנו בארץ מצרים או במדבר הזה לו מתנו. ג. ולמה ידוד מביא אתנו אל הארץ הזאת לנפל בחרב נשינו וטפנו יהיו לבז הלוא טוב לנו שוב מצרימה. 1. All of the congregation lifted their voice and the nation wept that night. 2. And all of the Children of Israel complained against Moshe and Aharon. And the entire congregation said to them: "If only we had died in the land of Egypt or if only we had died in this desert! 3. So why is HaShem bringing us to this land to fall by the sword, with our wives and our children to become the spoils of war? Will it not be better for us to *return to Egypt?*"

	2.	3.
SHEMOS 14 AT THE SEA OF REEDS *(cont.)*		
BEMIDBAR 11 GRUMBLING ABOUT THE MANNA *(cont.)*		
BEMIDBAR 14 THE SPIES *(cont.)*	ד. ויאמרו איש אל אחיו נתנה ראש ונשובה מצרימה. 4. And the men said to each other, "Let us appoint a leader and return to Egypt."	ה. ויפל משה ואהרן על פניהם לפני כל קהל עדת בני ישראל. 5. And Moshe and Aharon fell on their faces before the entire populace of the congregation of the Children of Israel.

10. Rejection on a Large Scale

	4.
SHEMOS 14 AT THE SEA OF REEDS	יג. ויאמר משה אל העם אל תיראו התיצבו וראו את ישועת ידוד אשר יעשה לכם היום כי אשר ראיתם את מצרים היום לא תסיפו לראתם עוד עד עולם. יד. ידוד ילחם לכם ואתם תחרישון. 13. And Moshe said to the nation: "Do not fear. Stand firm and view how HaShem will save you today, for after you have seen the Egyptians today, you will never see them again. 14. HaShem will war on your behalf, while you remain still."
BEMIDBAR 11 GRUMBLING ABOUT THE MANNA	טז. ויאמר ידוד אל משה אספה לי שבעים איש מזקני ישראל אשר ידעת כי הם זקני העם ושטריו ולקחת אתם אל אהל מועד והתיצבו שם עמך. 16. And HaShem said to Moshe: "Gather to Me seventy of the elders of Israel, men whom you have known to be elders of the nation and its authorities, and take them to the Tent of Meeting, where they will stand with you."
BEMIDBAR 14 THE SPIES	יא. ויאמר ידוד אל משה עד אנה ינאצני העם הזה ועד אנה לא יאמינו בי בכל האתות אשר עשיתי בקרבו. יב. אכנו בדבר ואורשנו ואעשה אתך לגוי גדול ועצום ממנו. 11. And HaShem said to Moshe, "How long will this people reject Me and how long will they have no faith in Me, after all of the miracles that I performed in their midst? 12. I shall strike them with plague and drive them away and make you [instead] into a nation greater and mightier than they."

On all three occasions, the people felt that there was an alternative to the present situation that would have been *better* than things were now. However, there is a vast difference between the first two and the third. In the first two, the people grumbled (1) as we all do occasionally, but had no thought of actually taking positive steps to remedy the situation. At the Sea of Reeds, they made no attempt to return to Egypt, and there was really not much that they could do about their dissatisfaction with the manna.

The people's reaction to the spies' pessimistic report was much different. They did not, as they had in the earlier two cases, contrast the wilderness existence with life in Egypt, but juxtaposed death in either Egypt or the wilderness against the slaughter that they anticipated if they were to enter the land. They made a sober judgment[4] that at all costs they must avoid the latter. They were therefore willing to defy the Ribbono shel Olam either by placing an idol at their head or by deposing God's chosen leadership in favor of Dasan and Aviram. Since under such circumstances wilderness existence would be purposeless and, moreover, impossible, they would return to Egypt and face the consequences (2).

Only this analysis can explain why Moshe and Aharon prostrated themselves (3) here and nowhere else during the first two years in the desert (verse 5).[5] The language of the verse makes it clear: *Moshe and Aharon prostrated themselves* BEFORE THE ENTIRE NATION OF ISRAEL. As R. Shamshon Refael Hirsch reads it, this implies a bowing to the will of the people. "We cannot," Moshe and Aharon[6] were saying, "lead you if you do not wish to be led."

What a sad picture! We had become a people for whom it made sense to substitute the leadership of Dasan and Aviram for that of Moshe Rabbeinu and Aharon. Small wonder that Yehoshua and Kaleiv tore their clothes

10. Rejection on a Large Scale

(Devarim 14:6). They mourned for a Klal Yisrael that had totally lost its bearings.

We must not permit all this analysis to make us forget the question that we posed at the beginning of this chapter: Are the two failings, the fact that the people chose to demand spies and the fact that they subsequently believed them, connected? Did the second follow from the first? We will leave this question to Chapter 12. We have some other business to take care of first.

Come! We have much to do.

II.

Stalking
the Truth Lurking
Beneath
the Facts

Writing history is tricky business. Knowing what took place is one thing. Knowing what *really* took place is quite another. Evaluating causes and effects, motives and expectations, recognizing the disparate potencies that may have left their mark—all this is not for the faint-hearted.

Historian and artist have much in common. The artist's genius lies less in the dexterity of his fingers or the range of his voice than in the depth and originality of his vision. Light and shadow, assonance and dissonance, the numerous other couplings that we might cite, all these whisper secrets to him which the rest of us are not privy to. So likewise with the historian. He is not a collator of facts; his quarry is not form but energy. He looks for a truth beneath the truth. He seeks the traces of eternity as they touch, lightly or heavily, upon the particular present that engages his interest.

In TaNaCh, the work of the historiographer is already done for us. Our task is to read carefully what is being said, to learn respectfully what is being taught and to pray for heavenly help in understanding correctly. Let us see what we can learn about the spies.

11. Stalking Truth Beneath the Facts

NaCh has two passages that revisit the story of the spies. There are sufficiently substantive differences between them to indicate that they are looking at what happened from two different perspectives. Let us take a look.

NECHEMIAH 9	TEHILLIM 106
טז. והם ואבתינו הזידו ויקשו את ערפם ולא שמעו אל מצותיך. יז. וימאנו לשמע ולא זכרו נפלאתיך אשר עשית עמהם ויקשו את ערפם ויתנו ראש לשוב לעבדתם במרים ואתה אלוה סליחות חנון ורחום ארך אפים ורב חסד ולא עזבתם.	יט. יעשו עגל בחרב וישתחוו למסכה. כ. וימירו את כבודם בתבנית שור אכל עשב. כא. שכחו אל מושיעם עשה גדלות במצרים. כב. נפלאות בארץ חם נוראות על ים סוף. כג. ויאמר להשמידם לולי משה בחירו עמד בפרץ לפניו להשיב חמתו מהשחית.
16. And they and our forefathers willfully made themselves stiff-necked and did not heed Your commandments. 17. And they refused to listen, and they did not keep in mind Your wonders that You had performed for them, and they made themselves stiff-necked and in their rebellion appointed a leader to return to their servitude. But You, forgiving God, gracious and merciful, slow to anger and filled with lovingkindness, did not abandon them.	19. They made a calf in Chorev, and they bowed to a molten image, 20. And they exchanged their Glorious One for the image of a grass-eating ox. 21. They forgot their Savior, Who had performed such great deeds in Egypt, 22. Wonders in the land of Cham, awesome acts at the Sea of Reeds. 23. And so He intended to wipe them out—if not for Moshe, His chosen one, who stood in the breach before Him to end His anger so that He would not destroy.

NECHEMIAH 9 *(cont.)*	TEHILLIM 106 *(cont.)*
יח. אף כי עשו להם עגל מסכה ויאמרו זה אלהיך אשר העלך ממצרים ויעשו נאצות גדלות.	כד. וימאסו בארץ חמדה לא האמינו לדברו.
	כה. וירגנו באהליהם לא שמעו בקול יְדוָד.
	כו. וישא ידו להם להפיל אותם במדבר.
18. They even made themselves a molten calf and said, "This is your god that brought you up from Egypt," and committed [other] terrible abominations.	כז. ולהפיל זרעם בגוים ולזרותם בארצות.
	24. They rejected a delightful land. They did not believe in His word,
	25. And they grumbled in their tents instead of heeding the voice of HaShem.
	26. So He raised His hand against them to cast them down in the wilderness,
	27. And to cast out their offspring amongst the nations and to scatter them amongst the lands.

Here is a list of the differences as far as I can make them out:

1. In Tehillim, the historical sequence is preserved. The story of the golden calf is told before that of the spies. In Nechemiah, the order is inverted.
2. Tehillim makes much of the punishment meted out to the people as a result of their lack of faith. It gives this equal billing (two verses) with the description of the sin. Nechemiah does not mention the punishment at all. On the contrary, the passage concentrates upon the mercy that God showed the people in spite of their rebellion.
3. Tehillim says nothing of the people's craven threat to return to Egypt, or of their rebellion against the leadership of Moshe Rabbeinu. Its criticism is directed only at

the obtuse spurning of the land. Nechemiah, on the other hand, stresses rebellion.[1] It goes so far in its preoccupation with that aspect of the story that it reports the wish that the people expressed as though they had actually carried it out.

I believe that the differences can be readily explained. The Tehillim passage is a song of praise to the Ribbono shel Olam for His unending kindness in the face of repeated provocation. Its presentation accords with this agenda. The Nechemiah passage is a confession of sin, and its approach to history conforms to this purpose.

Here is some textual body for this assertion.

I am constantly surprised, and not a little ashamed, at the superficiality with which I understand—or do not understand—verses that I recite constantly in *davening*. Too frequently I do not think sufficiently about the significance of each word. I have said *Hodu—Give thanks to HaShem for He is good, for His lovingkindness is* FOREVER—countless times without ever asking myself seriously what the implications of *forever* might be. Tehillim 106 begins with this verse, and even a cursory glance at the contents reveals the precise meaning. This chapter of Tehillim is a litany of the many sins that we committed throughout our history, and celebrates how, in spite of everything, the Ribbono shel Olam never gave up on us. The lovingkindness of the Ribbono shel Olam is indeed *forever*.

Chapter 9 in Nechemiah sets itself a different task. It follows immediately upon the deeply moving account of the first Rosh HaShanah that the returnees celebrated after the protective walls around Yerushalayim had been built. Ezra reads to them from the Torah scroll and awakens in them the realization that there is much that needs to be corrected in their Jewish lives. They are persuaded that their immediate obligation is to prepare for Succos, and they throw themselves into that task with all their energies. Immediately after the holiday, however, they return to their somber mood and, on the very first appropriate day, the twenty-fourth of Tishrey (the day following *Isru Chag*), they proceed with the necessary self-examination.[2]

The first verse reads, *On the twenty-fourth day of this month, all of Israel gathered for a fast, covered in sackcloth with earth scattered over them.* This sentence sets the tone for the rest of the chapter—which, as we have said, is a long and apparently deeply felt confession.

Here is our thesis: The worshipper, intent upon expressing his gratitude to God, sees things from a different perspective than the penitent digging around in the secret crevices of his soul. The former would have no reason to tell his story in any other than the correct sequence.[3] For the penitent, however, chronology is the least of his worries. He is interested in the murky depths within himself; he is trying to discover drives and motives that up to now may have been hidden from him. For him, it is quite possible that a later event will throw light upon an earlier one. The chaotic telling of his tale is a reflection of the chaotic state of his inner life. As he contemplates the sin of the spies, he realizes that the negative traits that he discovers can also serve to explain the sin of the golden calf.

Our first problem has been satisfactorily solved.

The penitent, eager to maximize his guilt, is not interested in any punishment he may already have been given. It is God's mercy in not exacting the full measure of what he might deserve that occupies his mind. He has abused that mercy, and for that there can be no excuse. His wickedness and his need for true penitence stand starkly and uncompromised before him. He is not a reporter bound to give an accurate account of what happened, but a human being writhing in remorse. A pedantic listing of what occurred is what he does *not* want. He looks for focus and for pain.

However, for the worshipper, contemplation of the punishment is a useful tool. It serves to underline the heinousness of the sin and therefore to put God's unbounded patience and love into sharp relief. There is no reason for him to leave it out, and every reason to give it play.

Our second problem has been satisfactorily solved.

For our purposes, the third issue is the most enticing. Somehow, these two sources must be made to yield what really went wrong in the episode of the spies. On the surface, the contradiction appears to be intractable. There seems to be little in common between a surly spurning of a delightful land and a spirit of rebellion against the leadership of Moshe Rabbeinu and Aharon.

Yirmeyahu 3:19 can help. The verse is not easy to translate. What I will offer is an approximation of what some of the commentators seem to suggest. Here is the verse.

ואנכי אמרתי איך אשיתך בבנים ואתן לך ארץ חמדה נחלת צבי צבאות
גוים ואמר אבי תקראי לי ומאחרי לא תשובי.

I wondered how I might raise you to a level of being true sons to Me, and so I gave you a delightful land, one which everyone would love to have, hoping that, in gratitude, you would call Me "Father" and never leave Me again.

It does not really matter whether my translation is accurate in every detail. The thrust is clear enough. God, as it were, had an agenda. He gave us the land that everyone else wanted, not because we *are* special but in order to *make* us special. Acceptance of the land would mean that we were taking it with all the strings attached. We would indicate our willingness to carry the awesome responsibility of being God's "children," of being familiar enough with Him to call Him "Father."

Armed with this new insight, we can see that the distance between rejecting the delightful land and rebelling against the leadership of Moshe Rabbeinu and Aharon is small indeed. If I am going to reject a close relationship with the Ribbono shel Olam because of the demands that such familiarity will make upon me, then the first thing that I will do will be to substitute Dasan for Moshe Rabbeinu and Aviram for Aharon. I will need someone who believes as I do, who will lead me back to Egypt rather than fixing his sights only on Eretz Yisrael.

We need not be surprised that Shlach's *let us appoint a leader* turns into *and they appointed a leader* in Nechemiah. Once rebellion is mooted, the damage is already done. For all practical purposes, the rejection of Moshe and Aharon's leadership was an accomplished fact.

We have made peace between our two sources and have found out that the evil that undergirded the fiasco was rebellion. However, we need to be a little clearer. Rebellion against whom?[4] Rebellion against what? The next chapter should move us closer to where we need to be.

12.

The Lure

of the Ordinary

One thing is certain. The episode of the spies played havoc with our history. Nothing was ever the same after that dreadful Tish'ah B'Av.

Why? What was there about the sin of the spies that made it more terrible than any of the other grumbling and shameful episodes that preceded it?

Of course, it may simply have been the straw that finally broke the camel's back after a long series of disappointments. BeMidbar 14:11—*how long will this people anger Me?*—and BeMidbar 14:22—*they tested Me these ten times*—seem to bear this out. Perhaps it was just that the measure of the Ribbono shel Olam's patience ran out.

However, the Midrash (Yalkut Shimoni, Tehillim 852) asserts that *among all the sins that the Israelites committed, the sin of the spies was the worst.*[1]

It seems that our Sages rejected the cumulative option. We will certainly need to examine how *they* read the two verses that we have just quoted in its favor. By the end of this essay, we will have a suggestion to make in that regard. But correct or not, it will not alter the fact that, now that we have discovered the above passage in the Yalkut, we will have to proceed on the assumption that the sin of the spies was somehow unique. This will color all our subsequent discussion here.

Let us return to our thoughts in the previous chapter. We concluded that the sin of the spies was one of rebellion. We wanted to know more exactly against what or whom this defiance was directed. We promised that we would devote the present chapter to this question. And so we must now begin to travel this difficult road.

We will do best to focus our attention upon BeMidbar 13:32. If we can make this verse yield its secrets, we will have gone a long way towards understanding what happened.

Here is the verse:

ויציאו דבת הארץ אשר תרו אותה אל בני ישראל לאמור הארץ אשר
עברנו בה לתור אותה ארץ אכלת יושביה היא וכל העם אשר ראינו
בתוכה אנשי מדות.

In their report to the Israelites,[2] they gave an evil report of the land upon which they had spied, telling them, "The land . . . is one which consumes its inhabitants. Moreover, the people whom we saw were huge."

There is a problem with the inner logic of this verse. If the land was really a dangerous place in which to live, if it was truly a land that *consumes its inhabitants*, then why were its inhabitants so huge? The two statements appear mutually contradictory.

Rashi and Ramban differ widely in their interpretations. Our focus will be on Rashi. However, we will first see how Ramban handles the issue, in order the better to understand the differences between them.

Ramban proceeds from the assumption that this part of the spies' report was simply not true.[3] The entire story was a fabrication. The spies claimed that the climate was so "harsh" (i.e., the land is "bad") that only the fittest could survive (i.e., the people were "few," but those few were "huge" and powerful). If we grant his premise, the two parts of the verse are perfectly coherent.

Rashi, however, following in the footsteps of our Sages, believes that the spies were telling the absolute truth. They had seen funerals taking place wherever they went. This caused them to take a very jaundiced view of the land. They did not realize that God had planned things this way in order to insure their safety. Everybody in the land was to be so busy mourning his dead that no one would have the time to wonder who these strangers might be.

However, this interpretation leaves the end of the verse dangling. How is all this connected with the fact that the people whom the spies met were unusually tall? Moreover, there is the contradiction that we noted above. How did the spies understand what they had seen? They should have asked themselves: why, if so many people became ill, were the rest so healthy? Why were the fruits of the land so huge and luscious when the people who should have enjoyed them were decaying in their graves?

I believe that I can offer an answer, although I would never claim that Rashi had this particular one in mind. Still, for what it is worth, I offer it here.

We live in an imperfect world. The most kindly natures can be entrapped behind a hideous or repulsive look; the profoundest evil can face the world with grace and beauty. There is an absolute incongruence between our inner and outer selves. Body and soul march to different music. Kuzari teaches us that this dissonance is not what the Ribbono shel Olam originally wanted.[4] At Sinai, when Yisrael for a short moment returned to what Adam had been before his sin (cf. Shabbos 146b), the blind began to see, the deaf to hear and the mute to speak. Inner life and outer form were to be and for a short time were one seamless whole. That is how the Ribbono shel

Olam created us and, if everything had worked out as it should have, that would have been the kind of world in which we lived.

Such uniformity between the inner and the outer spheres could, in a perfect world, be expected also from the land, particularly from Eretz Yisrael, God's very own. We would expect that a land blessed with spectacular physical properties would also harbor spectacular *spiritual* energy within itself. Certainly we would suppose that here was a place in which spiritual growth could flourish in an abundance unequaled in less favored areas.

Let us now imagine that wherever we looked in this land, people were dying. How would we interpret that? The answer seems clear. We would suppose that the spiritual virtuosity that all this energy demanded from its inhabitants was simply beyond them. They were unable to be as good as they were tall. And so they died. They died because gigantic greatness eluded them. They died because they were ordinary in a land in which the ordinary was simply not good enough.

The spies felt sure that they had the measure of God's land. Not for nothing did it flow with milk and honey. It was not for nothing that its people were so huge. The robust health that everything in this land exuded was a death knell for the spiritually timid. At last, they must have thought, they understood the strings that were attached to this desirable land that lay so welcoming at their feet. They understood what it takes to be able to say "Father" to God (see Chapter 11).

And they wanted none of it. Because its people were huge, this was a land *which consumes its inhabitants*. And, again, they wanted none of it.

Theirs was a rebellion of smallness against grandeur and challenge. They knew and felt comfortable with the gourds and cucumbers of Egypt. These, for them, were a perfect fit. They knew nothing of, nor did they care to find out about, the exhilarating battles of the spirit that would take them to new frontiers and open new worlds to them.

What do you, dear reader, think of all this? It seems to make sense, does it not?

Now, let us not permit the excitement of our explorations to make us forget the reason for which we undertook them. We need to discover how our Sages, who seem to reject the idea of cumulative guilt, deal with the verses that seem to affirm it. We are now in a position to suggest an answer.

These verses may well mean the following. The Ribbono shel Olam is looking back upon all the many disappointments that have punctuated the eighteen months since we left Egypt. As each disappointment occurred, He had treated it in isolation, forging appropriate reactions—forgiveness or punishment—on an individual basis. No general state of affairs was postulated. But the sin of the spies changed that. God then decided that everything that had happened had been part of a pattern, and that the people simply did not measure up. The shortfalls in faith and trusting acceptance that the earlier sins had revealed were not aberrations in the life of an otherwise healthy people but a part of the normal smallness of the small. The evidence that these people simply did not make the grade could no longer be ignored.

We have one other piece of unfinished business left over from Chapter 10. There we wondered whether the two failings—that the people chose to demand that spies be sent and that they subsequently believed them—were connected. We can now see that they were of one piece. The people were terrified of the challenges of the unknown. They wanted no part of entering the land miraculously, and they felt their fears confirmed by the report that the spies brought back. They had no stomach for the whole enterprise. Better, much better, to return to the pleasant life of the Egyptian gentry.

Sad, is it not?

Still, not everything was negative. Let us spend a few moments thinking about the *ma'apilim*, the Jews who insisted on entering the land on their own, desperate souls refusing to make peace with the verdict that had been pronounced against them, who thought that they could rewrite history. They failed and they died, but they left us with an important legacy.

Here is the Torah's account.

וישכמו בבקר ויעלו אל ראש ההר לאמר הננו ועלינו אל המקום אשר אמר ידוד כי חטאנו. ויאמר משה למה זה אתם עברים את פי ידוד והוא לא תצלח. אל תעלו כי אין ידוד בקרבכם ולא תנגפו לפני איביכם. כי העמלקי והכנעני שם לפניכם ונפלתם בחרב כי על כן שבתם מאחרי ידוד ולא יהיה ידוד עמכם. ויעפלו לעלות אל ראש ההר וארון ברית ידוד ומשה לא משו מקרב המחנה. וירד העמלקי והכנעני הישב בהר ההוא ויכום ויכתום עד החרמה.

[After hearing that they were all to die in the wilderness,] they arose in the morning and trekked to the top of the mountain as if to say, "We are ready! We will go up to the place of which God spoke, for [we admit that] we were wrong."

But Moshe Rabbeinu said to them, "Why will you not obey God? This move cannot succeed. Do not go up, for the Ribbono shel Olam is not in your midst. [Only by being obedient now and accepting your fate] can you avoid death at the hands of your enemies. [You must realize that] the Amalekites and the Canaanites will wipe you out. Now that you have repudiated God, He will no longer be with you."

But still, they forced their way to the mountaintop. However, the Ark of the Covenant and Moshe Rabbeinu made no move to leave the camp.

12. The Lure of the Ordinary

The Amalekites and the Canaanites who dwelt upon that mountain came down to destroy them, [and] ground them down utterly.[5]

It is a strange story, is it not? In saying *we were wrong*, the people were apparently repenting. They realized their mistake and sincerely regretted it. What made Moshe Rabbeinu so certain that the Ribbono shel Olam would not accept their penitence? He, if anybody, would know the power of repentance. With his fervor and refusal to capitulate following the sin of the golden calf, he had turned God's statement, *I refuse to go with you*, into *My Presence will go* [*with you*]. Had Moshe Rabbeinu suddenly lost his faith in repentance?

There is something very significant about repentance that we need to get clear. Although repentance can do a great deal, it cannot change the facts on the ground. If I have killed somebody and subsequently subject myself to all the rigors of Rabbeinu Yonah's *Sha'arey Teshuvah*, I will be forgiven, but my victim will not be restored to life. After eating from the Tree of Knowledge, Adam became the paradigmatic penitent, but he was not readmitted to Gan Eden. Reuven displayed an exemplary repentance, but the rights of the first-born did not revert to him. And the list goes on.

To understand what was happening here, I will quote myself from Chapter 9.

Man can live under the direct stewardship of the Ribbono shel Olam, or he can decide to go his own way. He and only he must decide. God does not impose Himself upon us. He is available to us should we want him, He will recede within Himself if we prefer to go it alone. The final few words in this passage are ominous. We can distance ourselves from the Ribbono shel Olam to the extent that *He leaves us to whatever nature has in store for us.*

This is what happened when, so long ago, we allowed our attachment to bland, impersonal nature to blind our souls. There was really no need to worry about sending spies. God did not need them and, if all had gone as it should, we would have entered the land as honored guests. It is we who decided that this was not the path we wished to follow. The moment we demanded spies it was clear that we had decided to prefer the exigencies of predictable nature to the unknowns of direct providence; that we had opted for independence, with all the horrors which this would entail, over submission.

Spies became a necessity.

God, as it were, sighed and commanded Moshe Rabbeinu to send spies.

We can put it this way: By opting for the perceived safety of the familiar and the ordinary over the frightening—although exhilarating—prospect of life lived directly at the Ribbono shel Olam's personal direction,[6] we drove ourselves out of our own Gan Eden. We became, tragically and unalterably, a people who were not at all what the Ribbono shel Olam had had in mind when he brought us out of Egypt. We were not ready to carry history on our backs in God's chosen land. Not until we had lived through, and been educated by, forty years of desert wandering would we be able to make up some of the lost ground. For the moment, we had lost our right to Eretz Yisrael, and the Ribbono shel Olam would make no move to help us get there by illicit routes.

So what is the important legacy that, as I claimed above, was left to us by the *ma'apilim*?

It is this: the *ma'apilim* were not evil, but overconfident. They did not realize how far Klal Yisrael had fallen, and they therefore misjudged the strength of their own spiritual muscles. But the time would come when, after our own trek through our exile in *the "wilderness" of the nations*,[7] we would be able to leap, as they were not, to heights that we had never imagined could be scaled.

Once more I quote myself, this time from Chapter 8 in my book *Beginnings* on Parashas Bereishis.

What did the *ma'apilim* think? Did they really believe that they could crash the gates to the Promised Land once the promise had been withdrawn? Would they alone, without divine help, be able to best the fearsome giants who had even now driven them to despair?

There was music in the *Hineinu* which was their rallying cry. We have, for want of better, translated it with the pallid "We are ready!" We hoped that the exclamation mark might breathe life into the boring English. It does not really work well. There is so much hope hidden in the Hebrew, so much determination and confidence in their newly discovered but yet unrealized holy power. They suddenly knew that greatness was, after all, within their grasp. They now understood that they had earlier failed in courage, had not dared to admit their own spiritual prowess, had lacked belief in what they could do if they were but determined to do it. From the depths of their despair, they had caught a glimpse of who they really were; they had come to know that nothing could really stand in their way.

It was too late. *This move cannot succeed.* Their moment of opportunity had sunk without trace, swallowed up in the maw of an unforgiving past.

Total despair.

But perhaps not quite so total. Perhaps their moment left a small trace after all. It took the discerning ear of the great R. Tzadok HaKohen of Lublin to hear what Moshe Rabbeinu really said. R. Tzadok was struck by the expression THIS *move cannot succeed,* which seems to carry an exclusionary connotation. The wording, *this* move cannot succeed, seems to hint of other attempts at gate-crashing that would meet with more positive results. Here is what he says [Tzidkas HaTzaddik 46]:

‮...והם לא הצליחו בזה מפני שאכלוה פגה כמו שאמרו ז"ל [סוטה מט:]‬
‮בעקבתא דמשיחא חוצפה יסגא, שאז הוא העת לזה ... ולכך אמר‬
‮להם משה, "והיא לא תצלח", נראה שעצה היא אלא שלא תצלח.‬
‮ודייק "והיא", שבכל מקום דרשו רז"ל "היא" ולא אחרת, שיש זמן אחר‬
‮שמצליח והוא זמננו שהוא עקבי משיח.‬

... they [the *ma'apilim*] were not successful in what they
did because the time was not yet ripe for such a move.
[But other times will come] as Chazal taught us, A mark
of the pre-Messianic era [*Ikvesa DeMeshicha*] will be an
increase in Chutzpah, meaning that at that time an ag-
gressive determination will bring results.

That is why Moshe Rabbeinu stressed the word *this*
in the phrase THIS *move will not succeed*. This implies that
their tactic was, in itself, reasonable. It was just that it
was premature. The choice of the word *this* is meant to
convey the idea that [although now they were doomed
to failure] a time would come when Chutzpah would be
crowned by success. That time has now come. It is the
Ikvesa DeMeshicha.

13.

The Spies and the Golden Calf Revisited

We have come a long way. We know much more about the episode of the spies than we did a while back. It is time to pick up where we left off in Chapter 6. There we began the important task of examining the differences between the sin of the spies and the sin of the golden calf. We did not yet know enough then to deal with niceties. We focused on the big picture. The time has come to revisit the subject, this time with more of an idea of where the truths that we are stalking might lead. Let us see whether we can find the right questions, for without these, the right answers will elude us.

Let us first examine what the Ribbono shel Olam said to Moshe Rabbeinu on each of these two occasions.

THE EPISODE OF THE SPIES	THE GOLDEN CALF
יא. ... עד אנה ינאצני העם הזה ... 11. "How long will this people anger Me ...?	ט. ראיתי את העם הזה והנה עם קשה עורף הוא. 9. "I have seen this nation, and behold, it is a stiff-necked nation.
יב. אכנו בדבר ואורשנו ואעשה אתך לגוי גדול ועצום ממנו. 12. I shall strike them with plague and drive them away and make you [instead] into a nation greater and mightier than they."	י. ועתה הניחה לי ויחר אפי בהם ואכלם ואעשה אותך לגוי גדול. 10. And now leave Me be, and My wrath will burn against them and destroy them, and I will make you into a great nation."

There are significant differences between the two passages. A careful reading yields the conclusion that, in spite of a surface similarity, they really have very little in common.

1. After the sin of the golden calf, the Ribbono shel Olam looks critically at the people (*I have seen*) and discovers something new about them (*and behold*). Their actions reveal them to be stiff-necked, something that had apparently not been evident before. Nothing like this happens in Shlach. In Shlach, God discovers nothing new about the people but expresses exasperation at their repeated failings.

2. There is an absolute difference between the *destroy* in the episode of golden calf and the *drive them away* in the episode of the spies.[1] Clearly, these disparate terms were chosen for a reason.

13. The Spies and Golden Calf Revisited

3. In the episode of the golden calf, Moshe Rabbeinu has a role to play. God tells Moshe to *leave Me be.* There is no parallel in the episode of the golden calf.
4. In the episode of the golden calf, there is mention of the Ribbono shel Olam's *fury.* The expression has no parallel in the episode of the spies.

A careful analysis of Rashi's remarks on the two passages will enable us to discover good and sufficient explanations for these differences. Here are the relevant comments:

THE EPISODE OF THE SPIES	THE GOLDEN CALF
רש״י במדבר יד:יב ואורשנו – לשון תרוכין. ואם תאמר מה אעשה לשבועת אבות. ואעשה אתך לגוי גדול – **שאתה מזרעם.** Rashi on BeMidbar 14:12, "And drive them away"—Expel them. And if you ask, what will I do about My oath to the patriarchs? "[I will] make you [instead] into a nation greater and mightier than they." For you are among the offspring [of the patriarchs].	**רש״י שמות לב:יג** לאברהם ליצחק ולישראל – אם לשרפה הם, זכור לאברהם שמסר עצמו לישרף עליך באור כשדים. אם להריגה, זכור ליצחק שפשט צוארו לעקידה. אם לגלות, זכור ליעקב שגלה לחרן, ואם אינן נצולין בזכותן, מה אתה אומר לי (פסוק י) ואעשה אותך לגוי גדול, **ואם כסא של שלוש רגלים אינו עומד לפניך בשעת כעסך, קל וחומר לכסא של רגל אחת.** Rashi on Shemos 32:13, "Avraham, Yitzchak and Ya'akov"—If they deserve burning, remember Avraham, who was ready to be burned to death for your sake in Ur Kasdim. If they deserve death [by the sword], recall Yitzchak, who stretched out his neck at the *akeidah.* If they deserve exile, recall Ya'akov, who was exiled to Charan. And if the Jews are not

THE SIN OF THE GOLDEN CALF
(cont.)

saved in the merit of the patriarchs, why do You tell me, *I will
make you into a nation greater* (verse
10)? *If a three-legged stool cannot
stand before Your wrath, how much
less so a stool with only one leg!*

In both cases, the Ribbono shel Olam announces that He proposes to build Moshe Rabbeinu into a great nation. Still, the two plans are radically different from one another.

After the sin of the golden calf, an entirely new nation was to be called into being. The patriarchs and their descendants were to disappear from Jewish history and Moshe Rabbeinu would be the sole founder of a new, "one-legged stool." The original three legs were to become a thing of the past. Things would begin afresh. Moshe Rabbeinu was to be the only patriarch of this new people.[2]

Later, in the episode of the spies, there is no thought of eliminating the past and beginning again from scratch. Avraham, Yitzchak and Ya'akov were to remain the patriarchs of Moshe Rabbeinu's descendants. The plan hinged on the fact that Moshe Rabbeinu himself was descended from the patriarchs.

Why? Why the change?[3]

We will soon find out the answer. It will explain the four divergences that we listed above. First, though, we must have a moment's patience. We must make a small detour.

We will visit BeReishis Rabbah 3:5.

13. The Spies and Golden Calf Revisited

ויבדל אלהים בין האור ובין החשך. כנגד ספר במדבר שהוא מבדיל בין
יוצאי מצרים לבאי הארץ.

God separated the light from the darkness. This describes the
Book of BeMidbar, in which those who left Egypt are
separated from those who were to come into the land.[4]

The Book of BeMidbar is divided into two by the in-
sertion of the couplet, *when the Ark traveled* ... and *when
it rested, he said* ... at 10:35 and 10:36. These two verses,
surrounded by two inverted letters *nun*, form a mini-
book, effectively separating the parts that precede them
from the parts that follow them, thereby making those
two parts into two discrete books.[5] The passage from
BeReishis Rabbah that we cited tells us that the earlier
"book" deals with those who left Egypt and the latter
one with those who were to enter the land of Israel.

Our Sages are telling us that these two groups are
sufficiently different from one another to warrant being
treated in two separate books. This has many ramifications. For us, its significance lies in the fact that
this places the episode of the golden calf (in the Book
of Shemos) with those who left Egypt, and the episode of
the spies with those who were to enter the land of Israel.

It seems logical to me to postulate that those who left
Egypt would be judged with an eye to the past. Are their
actions consistent with the great deliverance that they
had experienced? Did they or did they not deserve to have
been taken out of Egypt? When we think about those
who were to enter the land of Israel, we need to ponder
a different question: Are these the people who ought to
be brought into the land? Are they strong enough to bear
the destiny of Klal Yisrael upon their shoulders?

This difference in approach yields the following: The
sin of the golden calf would be considered a sin, a failing
to live up to the standards that these Jews' miraculous
past demanded of them. Sins call for punishment.

By contrast, the sin of the spies would have to be judged by a different standard. Perhaps we can go so far as to say that the term *sin* is a misnomer for what happened there.[6] Most people, even those who think of themselves as having a strong faith, would probably feel fear if a pit bull would suddenly jump its constraints and come for their throats. To be reckoned among those small in faith is not sinful. It is a mark of smallness, but that is all.

When the Ribbono shel Olam said, *I shall strike them with plague and drive them out,* He may not have meant this as a punishment at all. It was a judgment that these people would not, perhaps could not, measure up to the task to which history had summoned them. The Ribbono shel Olam was saying that He trusted Moshe Rabbeinu to educate his descendants towards the requisite greatness. For all the others, it was simply too late.

Let us test this theory by examining its impact upon the four differences in wording between the episode of the golden calf and the episode of the spies that we noted above. If this theory provides a reasonable explanation for these different perspectives, it will gain a considerable measure of credibility.

THE FIRST DIFFERENCE. As a result of the episode of the golden calf, the Ribbono shel Olam "discovers" that the Jews are *a stiff-necked people.* How? There seems to be nothing in the story that points to an unreasonable obstinacy. If asked to pinpoint the people's fault, we might suggest an insufficient trust in Moshe Rabbeinu's promise to return. Perhaps we would criticize a too-precipitous rush to find a solution to the problem as they perceived it. Obviously, we would feel that in asking Aharon to "make" a leader for them, they erred grievously. All this is true, and clearly we would not want to minimize the people's culpability. But we would not, on the face of the matter, regard obstinacy as their failing here.

13. The Spies and Golden Calf Revisited

It seems to me that in order to understand the accusation that we were *stiff-necked*, we must resort to the passage by Ramban at the end of Bo (13:16). He believes that the miracles that precipitated Pharaoh's capitulation, particularly the ten plagues, were all designed to teach fundamental truths about the Ribbono shel Olam: that He exists; He created the world; He knows and cares about what is going on in human society; He has the power to override nature and uses it; and so on.

We would have expected that the Jews, as did the Egyptians, would have absorbed these lessons. Had they done so, they could never have erred as grievously as they did. That the Israelites made the golden calf, that they even served it, marked them as refusing obstinately to relinquish any of their earlier ideas. They were so addicted to idol worship (see Yechezkel, Chapter 20) that they resisted ideas that made such service laughable.

The Ribbono shel Olam "discovers" that the covenant that He had made with these people had rested upon false assumptions. The best thing would be to erase the past and start once more from the beginning. The descendants of Avraham, Yitzchak and Ya'akov had become an irrelevancy. Moshe Rabbeinu must lay new foundations.

THE SECOND DIFFERENCE. None of this was applicable in the episode of the spies. Idol worship is a sin; terror of being slaughtered in battle is not.[7] We can certainly understand the people's fears when we consider that a little more than a year earlier they had still been enslaved in Egypt. There is obviously a limit to what might have been expected from people such as these.

Still, an absence of blame does not alter the fact that these people were simply not ready to enter the land. Accordingly, the Ribbono shel Olam "distanced" them. They would not enter the land; their children would.

THE THIRD DIFFERENCE. Moshe Rabbeinu is a party to what is happening in the context of the episode of the golden calf because the issue is whether or not he is to be the patriarch of a new nation. In the case of the spies, however, no change in his status is contemplated.

THE FOURTH DIFFERENCE. In the context of what we have written, this divergence is self-explanatory.

Our careful analysis of the text has yielded gratifying results. There is no reason to suppose that we cannot go further. Come, let us see whether we can examine some of the other textual oddities in the episode of the spies and extract new and significant insights from them.

14.

The Tragedy
of the Generation
of the
Wilderness

Before we take up the challenge that we presented at the end of the last chapter, let us look back one more time to the generation of the wilderness. Their lack of heart when it counted most condemned them to oblivion. Their children, not they, would be active players in our history. Those who had left Egypt had only one more task ahead of them: to dig their graves, lie down in them and die.[1]

How does our tradition look back upon these tragic figures?

Let us learn Sanhedrin 110b.[2]

תנו רבנן: דור המדבר אין להם חלק לעולם הבא, שנאמר . . . אשר נשבעתי באפי אם יבאון אל מנוחתי, דברי רבי עקיבא. רבי אליעזר אומר: באין הן לעולם הבא, שנאמר אספו לי חסידי כרתי בריתי עלי זבח. אלא מה אני מקיים אשר נשבעתי באפי – באפי נשבעתי, וחוזרני בי. . . . י.

אמר רבה בר בר חנה אמר רבי יוחנן: שבקה רבי עקיבא לחסידותיה, שנאמר הלך וקראת באזני ירושלים לאמר. . . זכרתי לך חסד נעוריך אהבת כלולתיך לכתך אחרי במדבר בארץ לא זרועה. ומה אחרים באים בזכותם, הם עצמן לא כל שכן?

R. Akiva maintains that the generation of the wilderness forfeited its share in the world-to-come. He bases this upon Tehillim 95:11 (which we recite on Friday night), where the Ribbono shel Olam says, *And in My anger, I swore that they would never reach My place of tranquillity.*[3]

R. Eliezer maintains that the generation of the wilderness did not forfeit its share in the world-to-come. He cites a verse in support of his opinion: *Gather to Me My faithful ones, who have confirmed My covenant with a sacrifice* (Tehillim 50:5).[4] And he explains why he is not concerned by the Tehillim verse that R. Akiva used. Yes, God swore *in His anger*. But He later changed His mind.

Rabbah bar Bar Channah cites R. Yochanan that "here, R. Akiva abandoned his customary generosity of spirit.[5] Had he wanted to, he could have found a way of 'awarding' the world-to-come to the generation of the wilderness." This, on the basis of Yirmeyahu 2:2: *I recall the affection of your youth, the love when you were betrothed to Me, how you followed Me into the wilderness, into an unsown land.* In this Yirmeyahu passage the Ribbono shel Olam promised the inhabitants of Yerushalayim that He would have mercy upon them because of the merit of Klal Yisrael's having followed Him into the wilderness. Does it not stand to reason that, if this merit was sufficiently great to help people who lived a thousand years later, it would surely help the very generation that had shown the heroism that Yirmeyahu describes?

Let us see to what extent we can understand both R. Akiva and R. Eliezer.

In regard to R. Akiva, I suspect that R. Yochanan's expression *R. Akiva abandoned his customary generosity of spirit* will help point us in the right direction. Let us spend a few moments tracing its provenance and meaning.

This passage is part of a larger one that speculates about three groups' prospects of attaining the world-

14. Tragedy of Generation of Wilderness

to-come: the generation of the wilderness, the Ten Tribes who split from the kingdom of Yehudah under Yeravam ben Nevat, and the young children of wicked Jews. In each case, the proofs and counterproofs are grounded in what appear to be rather loose interpretations of various verses. I would like to know something about the background of these discussions. And yet, why not just leave it all to the Ribbono shel Olam, Who knows the correct meaning of each verse and Who will act accordingly?[6]

I suspect that none of the disputants had any thought of influencing the decisions of the Ribbono shel Olam. Rather, they were expressing differing opinions about the religious and historical significance of the spies, the Ten Tribes and the young children of wicked Jews. To use typical yeshivah language, rights to the world-to-come are used only as a *siman*, an identifying factor. When R. Akiva asserts that the spies and the Ten Tribes are excluded from the world-to-come, he is simply expressing his opinion that their failings were so heinous that there simply could not be any forgiveness. His disputants felt otherwise.

Clearly, such opinions are rooted in a more general outlook. The seriousness one ascribes to any dereliction on the part of Klal Yisrael will depend on prior assumptions. One's perception of Klal Yisrael in its relationship to the Ribbono shel Olam and of the imperatives that govern its journey through history, the love one harbors for it, the kinship one feels with it—all these and many more factors will play a role in forming one's assessment. It is this necessarily subjective involvement that gave R. Yochanan the right to invoke R. Akiva's generosity of spirit.

Let us spend a little time analyzing this passage. Our general thesis does not really require it. Still, how can we tear ourselves away from a passage in the Talmud that tells of R. Akiva's love for Jews? If he loved us,

99

we certainly love him. Let us try to understand how
R. Yochanan knew that R. Akiva normally displayed a
special generosity of spirit and that he abandoned it only
concerning the generation of the wilderness and (as the
passage there subsequently develops) the Ten Tribes.
Once we understand all this well, we will be ready
to tackle the much harder question: why, in fact, was
R. Akiva inconsistent? Why did his generosity of spirit
not persuade him to interpret the relevant verses in such a
way that the spies and the Ten Tribes would merit a portion in the world-to-come?

We need to ask a very fundamental question. We have
already learned that we have three issues: the spies, the
Ten Tribes and the young children of wicked Jews. In
the first two cases, the spies and the Ten Tribes, R. Akiva
maintains that they do not merit the world-to-come. In
the third case, he argues that they do. Regarding these
first two cases, R. Yochanan believes that R. Akiva's decision was out of character. Why? Why not deduce from
the *two* cases in which he withholds the world-to-come
that he was *not* of a particularly generous spirit? Why not
maintain that the third case must somehow have been
different?

Our task begins with an analysis of the third case. We
will find that only an extreme generosity of spirit could
have persuaded R. Akiva to reach the conclusion that he
did.

Here is the passage.

קטני בני רשעי ישראל אין באין לעולם הבא, שנאמר כי הנה היום בא
בער כתנור והיו כל זדים וכל עשה רשעה קש ולהט אתם היום הבא
אמר ה' צבאות אשר לא יעזב להם שרש וענף. שרש, בעולם הזה, וענף,
לעולם הבא, דברי רבן גמליאל. רבי עקיבא אומר: באים הם לעולם
הבא, שנאמר שמר פתאים ה', שכן קורין בכרכי הים לינוקא פתיא.
ואומר גדו אילנא וחבלוהי ברם עקר שרשוהי בארעא שבקו. ואלא מה
אני מקיים לא יעזב להם שרש וענף, שלא יניח להם לא מצוה ולא שיורי
מצוה.

14. Tragedy of Generation of Wilderness

The following are the words of Rabban Gamliel.

The young children of wicked Jews will not attain the world-to-come. As the verse states, *Behold, the day comes, burning like an oven, when all the willful, all who do evil, shall be straw, and the coming day will set them aflame, says HaShem Tzevakos, so that neither root nor branch will be left of them* (Malachi 3:19). ("Root and branch," Rashi teaches us, refers to the children of the wicked.)

"Root" means [that they will not live in] this world, and "branch" [that they will not enjoy] the world-to-come.

But R. Akiva disagrees and asserts that they *will* attain the world-to-come. And he relies on the verse *HaShem guards the* Pesa'im *(literally, the foolish)* (Tehillim 116:6). Now there are places where people use the word *Pasia* for *child*. Assuming this meaning for *Pesa'im*, we can render the Tehillim verse to yield that *HaShem guards the children*.

In addition, another verse states, *Cut down the tree, thereby destroying it—but still, allow the roots to remain in the ground* (Daniel 4:11). So we see that the roots=children are to remain.

However, if that is the case, how do I understand the verse that states *neither root nor branch will be left them*? That latter verse means that [the wicked] will not have left for themselves any mitzvah or remnant of a mitzvah.

Rabban Gamliel cites a verse that quite clearly supports his position. The *evil* are obviously the wicked people of whom he and R. Akiva are speaking. *Root and branch* refers to their children, and the double expression indicates that they will be lost not only in this world but also in the next. Everything seems straightforward and one would think that everyone could agree.

But R. Akiva does not accept Rabban Gamliel's proposition. Not because he takes exception to Rabban

Gamliel's interpretation. Why would he? It is in no way forced, and R. Akiva does not dispute its cogency. It is true that in the end he will offer other meanings for *root* and *branch*. However, he will do so only because the two verses that he cites to bolster *his* position leave him no choice.

His rejection of Rabban Gamliel's way of learning the verse will be only as strong as the two sources that he musters.

Let us examine those sources.

The first comes from Tehillim 116:6: *HaShem guards the Pesa'im*. R. Akiva insists that this phrase contradicts Rabban Gamliel. Since God looks after the *Pesa'im*, it is clear that they attain the world-to-come. But who are these *Pesa'im*? R. Akiva's sole basis for assuming them to be children is the fact that in certain areas people used *Pasi'a* to mean *child*.

But R. Akiva must know that none of this carries much weight in discovering the sense in which David HaMelech had used the word a thousand years earlier. All languages change as time goes by, and the fact that a word was used in a particular way in his time cannot really tell us how David HaMelech might have used it. There are dozens, probably hundreds, of ways in which Mishnaic Hebrew differs from the Biblical.[7]

And we know that David HaMelech knew the basic meaning of the word *Pesi* (singular of *Pesa'im*). See, for example, Tehillim 19:8, where he described Torah as follows: *the testimony of HaShem is reliable, giving wisdom to the* Pesi. He meant that Torah brings wisdom even to the foolish and the gullible. So why should we assume that he meant anything else in Tehillim 116? Moreover, even if we were to grant that R. Akiva's interpretation is possible, it most certainly is not necessary. How, then, can it be used to refute the simple and natural translation offered by Rabban Gamliel?

14. Tragedy of Generation of Wilderness

R. Akiva's second proof comes from Daniel 4:20. An angel descended from heaven and announced, *Cut down the tree, thereby destroying it—but still, allow the roots to remain in the ground.* Rashi explains that R. Akiva sees the "roots" as symbolizing the children, and that the message was that although Nevuchadnetzar was to lose his kingship, his children and descendants would nevertheless succeed him on the throne.

But surely it seems counterintuitive to picture children as the "roots" of the father. Would it not be more natural to see them as his fruits? Even if we accept Rashi's interpretation of the angel's message, namely that Nevuchadnetzar's children would inherit his throne, it would still be unnecessary to translate the verse as does R. Akiva. It would seem more logical to have the roots stand for the dynasty from which the kingship of each individual monarch flows. In that case, the angel is saying that although Nevuchadnetzar the man is being punished, the dynasty remains unaffected, and consequently there is nothing to prevent his children from ascending the throne. Interpreted thus, *roots* do not refer to children, and so the verse would have no bearing upon R. Akiva's disagreement with Rabban Gamliel.

In short, one has the impression that R. Akiva was so determined to see only merit in the Jewish people that he cast around for any source, even one that needed to be nudged a little to accomplish the purpose. And so we can understand R. Yochanan when he says that R. Akiva's *generosity of spirit* ran away with him in his ruling concerning the young children of wicked Jews.

That established, R. Yochanan wonders why R. Akiva would not have done the same when the question revolved around the spies and the Ten Tribes.

Let us put the Ten Tribes aside and concentrate upon the spies, who are the focal point of our research. Let us analyze the verse from Yirmeyahu that R. Yochanan thought might have satisfied R. Akiva, had he been functioning with his normal generosity of spirit: *I recall the affection of your youth, the love when you were betrothed to Me, how you followed Me into the wilderness, into an unsown land.*

At first sight, R. Yochanan's question is strong indeed. The verse that he cites does yield the assessment that he claims, and, moreover, without any labored interpretation. His reading is absolutely straightforward. Of course, the verse in itself proves nothing without the logical inference that the Talmud makes, but that too should not present any problem. The argument is elegant and simple and, as far as we can see, irrefutable. In fact, we wonder why R. Yochanan had to invoke R. Akiva's ruling in the case of the young children of wicked Jews. Even if we didn't think of R. Akiva as being particularly generous of spirit, he would still presumably have agreed with R. Eliezer that although HaShem had initially been angry, He later changed His attitude.

The truth is that R. Yochanan's challenge from Yirmeyahu is not only good, it seems too good to be true. It is so logical that it creates a problem not only for R. Akiva but also for R. Eliezer. Namely, why did R. Eliezer cite a verse—*Gather to Me My faithful ones, who have confirmed My covenant with a sacrifice*—that, if it yields his conclusion, does so only with a certain degree of interpretation (i.e., determining who *those who have confirmed My covenant* are)? Why did R. Eliezer not instead use R. Yochanan's argument—which, as we have shown, is so much simpler?

The answer is clear. R. Eliezer did not use R. Yochanan's argument because it seems to suffer from a fatal flaw. The *affection of your youth* that Yirmeyahu invokes in favor of the hapless generation of the Destruction was indeed an act of supreme heroism—but it was performed by those who left Egypt, by the Jews before they failed the test of the spies so dismally.

14. Tragedy of Generation of Wilderness

Had the Jews in the desert continued to maintain the mindset in which they had followed the Ribbono shel Olam unquestioningly into the wilderness, they would never for a moment have asked for spies to be sent into the land. But they were no longer the same people. Something dreadful had happened to them. How, then, could the merit of *how you followed Me into the wilderness* help a people who resisted the Ribbono shel Olam's summons to walk with Him into Eretz Yisrael?

R. Yochanan certainly understood that it was for this reason that R. Eliezer had not invoked the argument from *I recall the affection of your youth*. Nevertheless, he thought that had R. Akiva not abandoned the generosity of spirit that he had demonstrated in his ruling concerning the young children of wicked Jews, he could have overcome this objection.

So much for the passage in Sanhedrin. However, we are still far from where we need to be. R. Yochanan chose to remark only that R. Akiva's stringency seemed to be out of character. He made no attempt to explain why R. Akiva would be guilty of such inconsistency.

In our context, we do not have this luxury. If we want to understand a little about the episode of the spies, we must take this final step. We must answer the following question: Why was R. Akiva, who had been perfectly happy to wink at certain difficulties in order to judge the young children of wicked Jews in the most favorable way possible, unwilling to do the same for the generation of the wilderness?

It seems to me that R. Akiva took his lead from the Ribbono shel Olam Himself. David HaMelech spells out the tragic picture for us. We need to study, and very carefully indeed, the final two verses of Tehillim 95.[8]

י. ארבעים שנה אקוט בדור ואמר עם תעי לבב הם והם לא ידעו דרכי.

יא. אשר נשבעתי באפי אם יבאון אל מנוחתי.

10. For forty years, I quarreled with that generation, saying, "They are a nation gone astray in their hearts, and they have not known my ways."

11. And in My anger, I swore that they would never reach My place of tranquillity.

What exactly is being said? More particularly, what does R. Akiva believe is being said?

We know from the passage in Sanhedrin quoted above that verse 11 lends itself to two interpretations. R. Eliezer was not fazed by the apparently straightforward statement that God swore to exclude the generation of the wilderness from world-to-come. He believes himself to be supported by the apparently unnecessary *in My anger*: God's oath had been made in anger, on the spur of the moment, and so we can assume that He later regretted it and relented.

But R. Akiva refuses to countenance this possibility. Why?

It seems to me that it is possible to read verse 10 in a way that precludes absolutely the possibility of reading verse 11 as does R. Eliezer. Let us see what verse 10 is meant to convey to us.

In what way did the Ribbono shel Olam quarrel with us during the forty-year period in the wilderness? Here is what Rashi says:

ארבעים שנה . . . נלחמתי בם ארבעים שנה להמיתם במדבר כי אמרתי תועי לבב הם.

. . . I battled against them for a full forty years in the sense that I made them die in the wilderness. I did this because I told Myself that they are a people who simply do not understand.

So God's forty-year quarrel with us expressed itself by making us die in the wilderness.

14. Tragedy of Generation of Wilderness

What a piece of history to have to live with! A huge black hole cutting thirty-seven years out of forty, sucking into its maw the lives and experiences of those who, alone among our forebears, had lived through the most formative events in our history. These were the people who could and should have educated the first children to be born in Eretz Yisrael. Think of the stories they could have told: of frogs croaking their way through Egypt, of seas splitting, of shofar blasts sounding. Think of the songs they could have sung, the dances they could have danced. All this lies buried in their unmarked desert graves. They, who should have triumphantly carried God's glory into Eretz Yisrael, became irrelevancies to be shunted aside in unseemly haste in order to make room for a new generation that, although sadly diminished, was appointed to replace them and to carry on the struggle.

Why do I say "in unseemly haste"? Let us listen to the Torah's words in Devarim 2:14–17.

יד. והימים אשר הלכנו מקדש ברנע עד אשר עברנו את נחל זרד שלשים ושמנה שנה עד תם כל הדור אנשי המלחמה מקרב המחנה כאשר נשבע ידוד להם.

טו. וגם יד ידוד היתה בם להמם מקרב המחנה עד תמם.

טז. ויהי כאשר תמו כל אנשי המלחמה למות מקרב העם.

יז. וידבר ידוד אלי לאמר.

14. Now thirty-eight years passed between the time that we left Kadesh Barne'a until we crossed Nachal Zered. It took these thirty-eight years for all the "warriors" to be cleared out of the camp in accordance with what God had sworn.

15. Moreover, God acted against them to rush them out of the camp, so that none of them should remain.

16. Only once all the "warriors" had died

17. Did HaShem speak to me....

I have taken some liberties with the translation in order to express what Rashi saw in this passage. Verses 14, 15 and 16 are an introduction to verse 17. There the word *speak* is used to describe the Ribbono shel Olam's mode of communication with Moshe Rabbeinu. In the Holy Tongue, *Speak* implies a direct, loving communication. But since the episode of the spies, *say*—a more distant and formal expression—had been used instead. Not until all those who had been tainted by the spies had died could the use of *speak* be justified once again.[9]

So much for the general thrust of these verses. Our interest focuses particularly on verse 15. Here is what Rashi offers: *The expression* GOD ACTED AGAINST THEM *implies that the Ribbono shel Olam acted against them so as to rush their deaths within the allotted time. This was necessary so that they should not, by their continued presence among them, hold back the next generation from entry into the land.*

This is what I had in mind when I used the expression "unseemly haste."

Why does the Ribbono shel Olam stress that his quarrel with Klal Yisrael lasted a full forty years? It seems to me that R. Akiva might well understand this stress upon the passage of time to make it impossible to understand the next verse as does R. Eliezer.

R. Eliezer claims that *in My anger* allows us to maintain that the Ribbono shel Olam backed down from His oath: Because he had sworn in anger, He therefore did not feel bound by it. R. Akiva believes that the earlier verse makes this interpretation impossible. Forty years is a long time. Had the Ribbono shel Olam really had second thoughts about the oath, there would have been plenty of opportunity to stop the dying. The fact that the death sentence upon that generation was carried out consistently year after year shows that the Ribbono shel Olam never wavered in His determination to carry out the oath that He had sworn.

14. Tragedy of Generation of Wilderness

There was apparently something particularly baneful about Klal Yisrael's involvement with the idea of sending the spies, in the first place, and the way in which, in the second place, they received the report that the spies brought back. No wonder that R. Akiva abandoned his usual generosity of spirit.

All this, I feel, tends to confirm the ideas that we have worked out in the past few chapters.

We are now ready to move on to the tasks that we set ourselves at the end of the previous essay.

15.

A World
Beneath
the World

I have thought long and hard about whether or not to write this essay. The last chapter was sad enough: too many failures, too many disappointments. We had to stand by and watch while even the large-hearted R. Akiva gave up on the generation of the wilderness. How much can we take? How much more must we wallow in our pitiful smallness? Perhaps we should follow the Torah's lead and cover over some failings. Not every weakness must be belabored.[1]

And yet, by looking away we may lose the chance to get at a truth that is much larger than any which we have grasped until now. We must soldier on.

Let us put the problem bluntly: R. Akiva tells us that the generation of the wilderness forfeited its portion in the world-to-come. That is no small matter. The Ribbono shel Olam Himself describes them as a people with an obtuse heart, a heart incapable of following a straight and true path. Things do not get much worse than that. But there is also another dimension, which we ignore at our peril. For another thirty-eight years, these same people lived on, embraced by the Clouds of Glory, sustained by the manna and by the miraculous Well of Miriam. That does not happen to people who are not loved.

How does all this fit together?

As I write, we read the parashah of Balak. It was the first time that I was struck by the shocking juxtaposition of the Bil'am story with that of the tragic encounter with the Moabite seductresses, which leads ultimately to the disgusting Pe'or worship. There is no softening bridge passage; the one follows the other with appalling immediacy. Bil'am leaves for home; the nation begins to fornicate. The description of Klal Yisrael that the Ribbono shel Olam places in Bil'am's mouth is completely at odds with the facts on the ground. What are we to do with this?

Here is an example of Bil'am's prophecy: *He has not gazed at sin within Ya'akov, nor has He seen anything deficient within Yisrael.* We will take the phrase as Rashi does and then compare it with what actually happens at the end of the parashah.

Here is what Rashi says.

לא הביט און ביעקב וגו'. . . . לא הביט הקב"ה און שביעקב, כשהן
עוברין על דבריו אינו מדקדק אחריהם להתבונן באוניות שלהם
ובעמלן שהן עוברין על דתו.
ה' אלהיו עמו. אפילו מכעיסין וממרים לפניו אינו זז מתוכן.
ותרועת מלך בו. לשון חבה ורעות. . . .

God does not concentrate upon Ya'akov's sins. Even when they do wrong, He takes no particular notice of it.

God always remains with His people. He never distances Himself from them. Nothing ever mitigates His love for them.

But that is not how things actually happen in Shittim. God's reaction there stands in stark contradiction to Bil'am's assertion. The Ribbono shel Olam certainly takes note of the people's transgression and, moreover, reacts to it with stern severity. Let us recall that the nation as a whole was the culprit here. The sinners were not a small group of hapless individuals but, at the very least, a large portion of the people. All of these are to be hanged, many more are to die by the plague. Only then will God's anger be assuaged.

None of this seems to be in consonance with *He has not gazed at sin within Ya'akov.*

Our Sages go way beyond what is demanded by the simple text in describing God's fury at what happened. 78,600 judges were involved in exacting punishment from the sinners,[2] and each sentenced a minimum of two people[3] to be hanged. We are thus talking about 157,200 gibbets. How, as they say in yeshivos, does this *shtim*, or correlate, with *He has not gazed at sin within Ya'akov*?

Something in us rebels at the idea that such a huge percentage of Klal Yisrael was indeed consigned to the gallows. Indeed, Ramban considers this totally unacceptable[4] and finds a way around it. I admit that all this has very little to do with the spies. Nevertheless, we will study Ramban's words on this episode carefully and lovingly because they are very much a part of the broad picture that we are attempting to portray.

Here is what Ramban says.

והנכון בעיני בעניין הפרשה, כי מתחלה נאמר (בפסוק ג) ויצמד ישראל
לבעל פעור ויחר אף ה' בישראל, כי יצא הקצף מלפני ה' החל הנגף.
והשם ברחמיו אמר למשה, שישפטו השופטים ויתלו הנצמדים ולא
יספה האף צדיק עם רשע, ומשה צוה כן לשופטים. וכאשר נאספו
כל העדה פתח אהל מועד לעשות כדבר משה ועוד הנגף הווה בהם,
והנה העז השמעוני הזה ויקרב אל אחיו את המדינית למרוד במשה
ובשופטים . . . והנה התחילו משה והשופטים לבכות, ויעמד פנחס
ויפלל ותעצר המגפה. ולא נדון אחד מכל העם ביד השופטים, כי השם
אמר (פסוק ד) והוקע אותם וישוב חרון אף ה' מישראל, וכבר שב אפו,
ולכך לא הזכיר הכתוב "ויעשו כן שופטי ישראל". ויתכן שתהיה כוונת
האגדה הנזכרת, לומר שיהיו ההרוגים לפי המצוה יותר מחמש עשרה
רבוא, לומר שהיו החוטאים רבים, אבל חסך עליהם עניין פנחס. . . .

15. A World Beneath the World

Instead of offering a translation, I will paraphrase:

The whole sorry episode elicited God's wrath, and a plague began to rage among the people. Now, when disaster strikes a community, the righteous will be as vulnerable as the wicked (see Bava Kama 60a). In order to protect the righteous, God told Moshe Rabbeinu to have the judges kill all the guilty people. This would assuage God's anger and, once it was done, the righteous would be safe. Immediately, everybody gathered in front of the Tent of Meeting, ready to do Moshe Rabbeinu's bidding. While all this was in progress, Zimri—in open rebellion—brought forward the Midianite woman and fornicated with her shamelessly for everyone to see. Pinchas, invoking the halachah that *zealots may strike at a man fornicating with a non-Jewish woman*,[5] killed them both. This act of appropriate zealotry appeased the Ribbono shel Olam, making it unnecessary to kill the other offenders. Accordingly, none of those who were due to be hanged were actually killed.

Ramban makes it simpler to live with this incident. We breathe a little easier; it did not really happen. However, he does not help us with our basic difficulty: How does the entire episode comport itself with Bil'am's *He has not gazed at sin within Ya'akov*?

There is another point that we ought to pursue. How can Pinchas's zealotry be traded against the punishment that the sinners so richly deserved? Ramban tells us the mechanics: these were to be killed in order to assuage God's anger; Pinchas, by doing what he did, assuaged God's anger; therefore, the death of the sinners was no longer required. But it is difficult to feel satisfied with this explanation. The mathematics works out, but our sense of fairness is offended. People who commit a capital crime are executed because justice requires that they be punished. Why should an act of zealotry, be it ever so praiseworthy, set aside that requirement?

Let us first state the obvious. The hanging that was to take place here was not to be in fulfillment of the normal death penalty. Ramban himself points out that that would have required the convening of a formal court, which did not happen. Moreover, the text itself indicates that this was something special. The Ribbono shel Olam said, *Hang them so that My anger will be assuaged.* He did not say, "Hang them because they have committed a capital crime and the halachah demands that they be killed."

What is going on here?

I have a suggestion to make; I offer it for what it is worth.

When the Ribbono shel Olam delegated Moshe Rabbeinu to tell the judges to kill the sinners, he said, *Take all the leaders of the nation and hang them before HaShem facing the sun....* There are three points here: 1. The sinners are to be hanged. 2. They are to be hanged *before HaShem.* 3. The hanging is to be done *facing the sun.* We will examine these points one by one.

1. Rashi explains as follows: Worship of Baal Pe'or is, of course, idol worship. The prescribed punishment for this is stoning, followed, according to the halachah, by hanging.[6] The requirement that the sinners be hanged is therefore in no way extraordinary. But in that case, there seems to be no valid reason why the hanging should be mentioned at all. Since it is simply subordinate to the stoning, without any significance of its own, Moshe Rabbeinu ought to have told the judges that the sinners were to be stoned. The subsequent hanging would have been self-understood.

2. What is meant by *before HaShem?* In what way would hanging the sinner be *before HaShem?*[7] Now it is interesting that in II Shmuel 21:6 we also have *they shall be hanged before HaShem.* However, there too we are at a loss to understand the significance. The source for hanging those

who are stoned is in Devarim 21:22, *hang him upon the gibbet.* There, nothing is said that would imply that the hanging is to be *before HaShem.*

3. The simple meaning of *facing the sun* is *for everyone to see.* I am not aware of any law that provides that regular hangings need to be conducted in public.[8] Indeed, the requirement that all should be in the open seems incongruous in light of the fact that in normal circumstances when people are hanged, they are immediately taken down because, as Devarim 21:23 teaches, *it is a disgrace to the Ribbono shel Olam that man who was created in His image should be hanging lifeless on the gallows.*[9]

I suggest that the passage from Ramban quoted above would not agree with Rashi that the sinners were to be hanged as a part of the stoning process. We recall that there were no properly convened courts consisting each of twenty-three judges. Each official acted on his own, and therefore no formal death sentence could have been imposed. The killing here was *sui generis*; it was self-justifying. Our problems with *before Hashem* and *facing the sun* will have to find their solution within the unique circumstances of this particular incident.

The explanation may well be as follows:

The service of Pe'or consisted of a particularly revolting procedure. The worshipper defecated and then cleansed himself upon a protrusion jutting out from the idol. Sanhedrin 64a tells this story: A gentile woman fell ill. She swore that if she recovered, she would express her gratitude to every idol in the world. She did recover, and set about fulfilling her vow. All went well until she came to Pe'or. When the priests told her what she was expected to do, she refused, declaring that she would rather die than engage in such filthy cultic practices. The Talmud then continues sadly, *You, Israel, do not have the same degree of sensitivity. Concerning you it is written, ". . . who were coupled to Pe'or." You cleaved to it as tightly as a lid is fixed to a jar.*

What a bitter censure. The rest follows of its own logic. People who have dropped out of humanity have *a fortiori* dropped out of Klal Yisrael. It is in this sense that the fornicators' hanging is described as *before Hashem—* that is, *for the sake of the Ribbono shel Olam.* His Klal Yisrael remains unblemished because these sinners have been expelled from its ranks.[10]

This can also explain the expression *facing the sun.* We could simply leave the meaning as *for all to see,* and it would make a great deal of sense. It was important that the expulsion of the sinners from the ranks of Klal Yisrael should be as public as possible. The more people knew, the less desecration of God's Name there would be and, moreover, the dreadful sight would have an enormous educational impact. People needed to know that it is no small matter to sink to the level to which these had descended.

There is, however, a second interpretation in Rashi, which, if we think it through, will confirm all that we have surmised.

Here are Rashi's words:

נגד השמש. לעין כל. ומדרש אגדה השמש מודיע את החוטאים, הענן
נקפל מכנגדו והחמה זורחת עליו.

Facing the sun means *before everyone.* [In other words, the executions were to be performed in public. That is the simple meaning of the verse. But now Rashi cites a Midrash Aggadah.]

It is the sun that identified the sinners. The Clouds of Glory, which surrounded the whole camp and placed it in the shade, folded over and allowed the sun to shine through upon the sinner.

Think of that! It is hard to imagine a more graphic illustration of what was really involved. Nowhere else do we find this particular method of identification. The Torah is not concerned with telling us how the Levites knew who had participated in the worship of the golden calf. Whatever method was used there could, one would suppose, just as well have been used here. But it wasn't. The sun was used. The lesson is clear. The Ribbono shel Olam was showing everybody that the sinners had dealt themselves out of Klal Yisrael. They were no longer surrounded by the Clouds of Glory. They were out in the sun. They were out in the wilderness. They were all on their own.

Let us get back to the questions that we posed at the beginning of this essay. Here they are once more:

1. The generation of the wilderness, those to whom R. Akiva had refused the world-to-come, nevertheless remained within the Ribbono shel Olam's embrace until their death. They were guarded by the Clouds of Glory, sustained by the manna, their thirst slaked by Miriam's well. We felt that this needed an explanation.

2. Bil'am's copious praise of Klal Yisrael appears to be contradicted by the facts on the ground. How can we maintain that *Hashem has not gazed at sin within Ya'akov* when just a few lines later we learn of 157,200 condemned to death?

3. How are we to understand Ramban's assertion that Pinchas's zealotry assuaged God's anger to the extent that it was no longer necessary to carry out the death sentences against the many thousands of other Pe'or worshippers?

This essay has already become longer than it should have been. Nevertheless, we will make one last, small excursus, which will help us to sum up our conclusions.

Bil'am refuses to give up. Although God had already refused him permission to accompany the first delegation, he tries once more. His hatred will not permit him to simply send the second delegation packing. Against all our expectations, God appears to be more positively inclined to Bil'am's insistence than He had been the last time. If Bil'am's visitors insist that they want him even though they know that he will not be able to curse the Jews, God says that he may go. Ramban is puzzled. Why would the Ribbono shel Olam permit this charade?

Here is Ramban's answer in Parashas Balak.

וכן היה החפץ לשם הנכבד מתחלה שילך עמהם, אחרי הודיעו אותם שלא יקללם ושיתנהג בענינים כאשר יצוה, כי הרצון לפניו יתברך שיברך את ישראל מפי נביא לגוים.

Once it had been made clear that Bil'am would not be permitted to curse and that he would be doing whatever he was commanded to do, God wanted Bil'am to accompany them. This, because it was God's wish that Israel should receive blessings by the mouth of him who was *the* prophet to the gentile nations.

Ramban introduces us to a concept of which I had never been aware before. Why was it important to the Ribbono shel Olam that we should be blessed by Bil'am? Since Ramban does not explain, we are left to our own devices.

Here is my suggestion:

Bava Basra 14b deals with the authorship of the various books that make up our TaNaCh. As part of the general discussion, we find the following: *Moshe Rabbeinu wrote his own book, the parashah of Bil'am and the Book of Iyyov (Job)*. Some Rishonim are disturbed by the mention of the parashah of Bil'am as a separate entity. They go so far as to suggest that the reference is not to the parashah that we know from the Book of BeMidbar. That would be part of *his own book*. Rather, Moshe Rabbeinu must have written a different book, one that has been lost to us, in which he elaborated upon the Bil'am story.

Rashi, however, takes the expression *the parashah of Bil'am* literally. He tackles the problem that the Rishonim raise in the following words: *Moshe wrote Bil'am's prophecies and parables, although they really had nothing to do with him, his Torah or his history.*

Rashi leaves us dangling. If the Bil'am saga does not really belong in the Torah, why is it there? Why permit access to an intruder who disturbs the otherwise harmonious cohesion of Moshe's book?

I believe that the parashah of Bil'am stands at the very fulcrum of world history. I believe that it is designed to foreshadow Yeshayahu's vision of the Messianic era (Yeshayahu 2:2), when—

נכון יהיה הר בית ידוד בראש ההרים ונשא מגבעות ונהרו אליו כל ...
הגוים. והלכו עמים רבים ואמרו לכו ונעלה אל הר ידוד אל בית אלהי
יעקב וירנו מדרכיו ונלכה בארחתיו כי מציון תצא תורה ודבר ידוד
מירושלם.

... the Beis HaMikdash will be firmly ensconced on the peak of its mountain, higher than all the hills. All the nations will flow towards it. They will call to one another, "Come, let us go up to the mountain of HaShem, to the temple of Ya'akov's God. Let them teach us His ways so that we may walk in His paths. For it is from Zion that Torah goes forth, the word of HaShem from Yerushalayim."

The nations of the world recognize that it is only from Zion that Torah goes forth, that the word of the Ribbono shel Olam can be found only in Yerushalayim. It was Bil'am, through his inspired visions, who laid the groundwork for this insight. The Ribbono shel Olam wanted us to be blessed by the prophet of the nations so that what Bil'am taught would become the property of all mankind. It is ignored, it is suppressed, it rankles like a low-level fever until it erupts into murderous hatred, but it is there. The time will come when it will flower into the sanctification of God's Name at the End of Days.

It is true that the parashah of Bil'am is an intruder into the Torah of Moshe. It is the Torah for the nations, which in its own right has no place there. But in the end it does belong there. What other purpose can our Torah have for us if not that through us, all of mankind will find its deliverance—*to rectify the world under the sovereignty of the Almighty?*[11]

We will now return to the three questions that we posed above.

We will begin with the second one. We were concerned with the fact that Bil'am's copious praise of Klal Yisrael does not seem to be borne out by the facts on the ground. Bil'am says that *Hashem has not gazed upon sin within Ya'akov,* yet the Ribbono shel Olam wants 157,200 Jews to be hanged because of the debacle at Shittim.

Now that we have understood the place that the parashah of Bil'am occupies in Moshe Rabbeinu's Torah, we may say as follows: The Ya'akov and Yisrael of whom Bil'am speaks when he says that the Ribbono shel Olam does not concentrate upon their sins is a conceptual ideal that spans the generations between Avraham Avinu and the advent of the Mashiach. It does not and cannot refer to any particular Jews at any particular time. It is to that Klal Yisrael that the nations of the Yeshayahu passage will one day flow. When Bil'am says that the Ribbono shel Olam does not take note of Ya'akov's sins, he means that the sins of any particular generation are seen as aberrations that do not affect the Klal Yisrael of history. Certainly, sinners will be punished, even when many thousands are involved. This fact is confirmed throughout TaNaCh. The Ribbono shel Olam does not wish to, nor will He, simply brush over delinquencies. However, that rule does not hold true for the Klal Yisrael of history. That entity cannot be touched by the failings of individuals. It remains, and will always remain, intact, in order to play its role in the world's rectification of which the prophets dreamed.

We wondered earlier why the generation of the wilderness—who, according to R. Akiva's harsh conclusion, lost their portion in the world-to-come—nevertheless remained in good standing until their deaths. The answer is simple enough. They, in contrast to the Pe'or worshippers, did not deal themselves out of Klal Yisrael. They sinned grievously and lost everything—everything, that is, which should have been theirs as individuals. Nevertheless, for them no Clouds of Glory peeled back in order to allow the baleful sun to mark them as outcasts. The clouds, the manna and the well were the Ribbono shel Olam's gift to the Klal Yisrael of eternity. In spite of their dereliction, the generation of the wilderness remained a part of that Klal.

We were, of course, most concerned with our third question. How are we to understand Ramban's assertion that the zealotry displayed by Pinchas assuaged God's anger to the extent that killing the other Pe'or worshippers was no longer necessary?

Here are my thoughts. You, dear reader, will judge whether you find them persuasive.

The halachah that *zealots may strike at a man fornicating with a non-Jewish woman* touches the Jewish essence at the very deepest level. This is so because it draws its energy from a sub-halachic stratum. Here let us turn our attention to Rambam's formulation of this halachah (Mishneh Torah Isurei Bi'ah 12:5):

אין הקנאי רשאי לפגוע בהן אלא בשעת מעשה כזמרי שנאמר ואת
האשה אל קבתה אבל אם פירש אין הורגין אותו, ואם הרגו נהרג עליו,

ואם בא הקנאי ליטול רשות מב"ד להרגו אין מורין לו ואע"פ שהוא
בשעת מעשה, ולא עוד אלא אם בא הקנאי להרוג את הבועל ונשמט
הבועל והרג הקנאי כדי להציל עצמו מידו אין הבועל נהרג עליו.

The zealot is allowed to kill the fornicators only while
they are actually engaged in the act. . . . If they have already separated, he is not permitted to kill them. If, in
spite of this, he kills them, he is a murderer and will be
condemned to death. Moreover, if the zealot asks the
court for permission to kill the fornicators, this will be
denied him even if they are still in the act. Not only this,
but if the fornicator kills the zealot before the zealot has
the chance to kill him, he is guiltless. He has the right to
kill the zealot to save his own life.

It is remarkable, is it not? The halachah that *zealots may
strike at a man fornicating with a non-Jewish woman* is not
halachah at all. Rather, it is a mandate to *ignore* the halachah. The court will not countenance this act. It is murder, and murder is not allowed. It is so clearly murder
that the fornicator is guiltless if, in self-defense, he kills
the zealot first. Nobody is forced to allow himself to be
murdered. The attack of the zealot is an act that, so we
might say, the Ribbono shel Olam understands, but for
which there is no room in the world of halachah.

It is as I have said. There is a substratum of Jewish action that derives not from what a Jew must *do,* but from
what a Jew must *be.* In the face of a terrible desecration
of God's Name, halachah must, so to speak, grit its teeth
and look away.

We can understand why the Ribbono shel Olam allowed Pinchas's act of zealotry to allay His anger. It
brought Him face to face with His Jews at the most el-
emental level. In the strait-laced world of halachah, the
Pe'or worshippers had indeed gone beyond the pale.
They had acted as Jews cannot act if they are to remain
Jews. However, Pinchas had discovered a Judaism of

15. A World Beneath the World

being, an untrammeled Judaism that is free to be itself, that asks no questions and makes no excuses because it knows itself to be—itself.

In such a world, there is room for even the Pe'or worshippers. The building above the ground had indeed been completely destroyed, but a subterranean foundation remained. There is hope that something strong and beautiful might yet arise from the rubble.

16.

Meeting Yehoshua and Kaleiv

The time has come to turn our attention to Yehoshua and Kaleiv. We have seen that the episode of the spies, in BeMidbar 14, turned our whole history on its head. Our relationship to Eretz Yisrael was compromised; the destruction of the first Beis HaMikdash became a foregone conclusion. The seeds of our exile were sown; the light of those who had left Egypt was eclipsed by the darkness of those who were to enter the land of Israel.[1]

If ever there was a blow that required healing, it was this. Now we know that the Ribbono shel Olam *does not hurt us without having already provided a corrective*,[2] and one must suppose that this was no exception.

If all this is true, it stands to reason that, to the extent that the blow was brought about by the ten spies who had lost their bearings, then the healing might well lie with Yehoshua and Kaleiv, who were a part of the group of sinners, yet who had stood firm.

Of course, this is a thesis that I cannot prove. Nevertheless, I will stick with it over the next few chapters in the hope that, once I have presented my case, you, dear reader, may be moved to agree. I am going to develop my thesis over a number of chapters. This will give us a chance to evaluate each stage carefully.

I shall begin by examining a phrase from BeMidbar 14 that does not at all stand at the center of the argument that I intend to make. Still, we should address it, even if it is no more than a matter of crossing a recalcitrant "t" and dotting a problematic "i." I want to whet your appetite for the chase by pointing to a possible interpretation of a difficult verse.

לו. והאנשים אשר שלח משה לתור את הארץ וישבו וילינו עליו את כל העדה להוציא דבה על הארץ.

לז. וימתו האנשים מוצאי דבת הארץ רעה במגפה לפני ידוד.

לח. ויהושע בן נון וכלב בן יפנה **חיו מן האנשים** ההם ההלכים לתור את הארץ.

36. The men whom Moshe Rabbeinu had sent to spy out the land and who returned and then, by slandering the land, made all the people grumble—

37. These men, the slanderers of the land, died of a plague before HaShem.

38. And Yehoshua bin Nun and Kaleiv ben Yefunneh *remained alive of those men* who had gone to spy out the land.

Verses 36 and 37 are clear enough. Our problem is with verse 38. It seems unnecessary to tell us that Yehoshua and Kaleiv did not die. The earlier verses had made it clear that only the slanderers were condemned. Why should these two have been in any danger?

Our first step must be to examine the meaning of the idiom *remained alive of those men*. I was able to find only one similar use in TaNaCh. That is in Shoftim 21:14, where the language is *women who remained alive of the women of Yavesh Gilead.*[3] As noted, a similar translation, that is, . . . *were not killed together with the others*, would be redundant here, since it has already been stated that only the slanderers were killed.

Rashi was troubled by our question and offers a midrashic interpretation (see Bava Basra 118b). But this rendering does not account for the parallel use in Shoftim.[4]

Perhaps we might consider the following.

Our Sages teach us that *once a destroying angel has been turned loose upon a community, he does not differentiate between the righteous and the wicked* (Bava Kama 60a.) The sense is that there are punishments that are directed against a communal body rather than against an individual. In such a situation, even the righteous within that community are vulnerable.

It may well be that the twelve spies had a collective identity. Yehoshua and Kaleiv were a part of that group, although, of course, they did not go along with the evil that the others perpetrated. This would explain Devarim 1:23, *I chose twelve men from among you, one man from each tribe.* The words *twelve men* would be superfluous if the spies would have been considered as individuals.

This seems to be confirmed in Shlach 14:6, when the verse says, *Yehoshua . . . and Kaleiv . . . WHO HAD BEEN AMONG THOSE WHO HAD SPIED OUT THE LAND, tore their clothes.* There seems to be no logic at all that would demand the phrase *among those who had spied out the land*, were it not in order to stress that, in spite of the fact that they distanced themselves from the other spies by tearing their clothes, they were still considered to be part of the group.

If all this is true, then it could serve as an explanation of the phrase *remained alive of those men,* which troubled us earlier. As a group, they were all slanderers of the land. Yehoshua and Kaleiv should also have been killed, since the forces of destruction had been turned loose upon them as a group.

Why were they not?

The answer may be as we suggested at the beginning of this essay. The Ribbono shel Olam may have deter-

16. Meeting Yehoshua and Kaleiv

mined that, since Klal Yisrael had been smitten because of the spies, the remedy for this blow should also come from within this group.

Of this, more in the following essays.

17.

Kaleiv I

ost of us, I think, conceive of Yehoshua and Kaleiv as a pair, standing shoulder to shoulder against the other spies. These two were good; the others were bad. They kept the faith; the others betrayed. In our mind's eye, we see them sticking together throughout the ordeal, strengthening one another and planning how they would act at the all-important moment when the whole group would be called upon to render an accounting of their travels.

Well, that is not the way it was. Contrary to our childhood impressions, we are going to have to learn to look at Yehoshua and Kaleiv with new eyes. A chasm separated them from one another. We are going to meet a serene Yehoshua, uninvolved, untroubled by doubts, going along because Moshe Rabbeinu sent him, but not really a "spy" at all. There was nothing particular that he expected to learn on this trip. The Ribbono shel Olam had said that the land was "good," and that closed the matter for him. The details that they all would uncover were precisely that: details that might help in small ways but had no impact on the larger picture.

17. Kaleiv I

The experiences of the Kaleiv whom we will get to know were anything but calm. He was a riven and conflicted man, very much a part of the group, casting about with desperate energy to find out where his loyalties lay. He, not Yehoshua, is the true hero of the story. The episode, as far as we can tell, left Yehoshua untouched. It propelled Kaleiv to the very center of Jewish history.

By now you, dear reader, may have begun to wonder whether this is a proper book for you to read. It all sounds strange and, to tell the truth, a little sensational. You may well be asking, "If there is any truth to all this, how come it is all new to me? Year after year we have read Shlach in shul and never picked up any of this."

I am, however, in deadly earnest. The story of the spies is one of those in which a placid enough surface disguises a roiling turbulence below. Those depths would remain hidden from us if our Sages and the commentators were not there to help us along. Let us wipe the slate of our memories clean and start again from the beginning. Our Sages exhort us that the words of the Torah should always seem new to us (Yalkut Shimoni, Mishley 937). Here is a good place to start.

The truth is that even a cursory reading of Chumash with Rashi in Shlach yields some indications that Yehoshua and Kaleiv played distinctly different roles in the drama. We recall that Moshe Rabbeinu changed Yehoshua's name in order to indicate, *May God protect you from falling in with the plots of the spies*,[1] but did nothing similar for Kaleiv. Kaleiv but not Yehoshua went to Chevron[2] to *beg God's help at the [Cave of] Machpeilah* that was situated there and it was he, not Yehoshua, who hushed the people in an attempt to turn the incipient rebellion around (13:30).

So it does seem that Kaleiv is not simply a second Yehoshua. Clearly, however, it will not do simply to realize what he was not. Let us try to gather a little more evidence, this time not from Shlach but from a passage in Yehoshua, to bolster our impressions and to move us forward towards a clearer understanding of the whats and whys of Kaleiv's role in the drama.

We are lucky that we have Kaleiv's own words to help us along our road of discovery. We fast-forward forty years. Moshe Rabbeinu has already died and Yehoshua has succeeded him. Kaleiv, no longer a colleague but a supplicant, comes to ask Yehoshua for permission to wrest Chevron from the gigantic people who were occupying it and to make it his own. He claims that Moshe Rabbeinu had promised it to him. He had gone there to pray and it was only right that it become his portion in the land.[3]

Here is the preamble to his request as it is recorded in Yehoshua 14:6–8.

ו. ויגשו בני יהודה אל יהושע בגלגל ויאמר אליו כלב בן יפנה הקנזי אתה ידעת את הדבר אשר דבר ידוד אל משה איש האלהים על אדותי ועל אדותיך בקדש ברנע.

ז. בן ארבעים שנה אנכי בשלח משה עבד ידוד אתי מקדש ברנע לרגל את הארץ ואשב אתו דבר כאשר עם לבבי.

ח. ואחי אשר עלו עמי המסיו את לב העם ואנכי מלאתי אחרי ידוד אלהי.

6. The tribe of Yehudah approached Yehoshua in Gilgal. Kaleiv said to him, "You surely remember what HaShem said to Moshe Rabbeinu at Kadesh Barne'a concerning me and concerning you.

7. "I was forty years old when Moshe Rabbeinu sent me from Kadesh Barne'a so that I might spy out the land. I brought him back an answer expressing what was in my heart.

8. "My brothers, however, those who went up with me, frightened the people. In spite of this, I remained loyal to HaShem."

17. Kaleiv I

We are of course immediately struck by the first person singular formulation that Kaleiv uses. We would certainly have expected that in talking to Yehoshua, with whom he had been twinned, he would use "we" instead of "I." In general terms, this usage supports our earlier suspicions that Kaleiv was and considered himself to be a loner.

Here are some thoughts concerning the specific language that he uses. In each of the three verses that we have quoted, Kaleiv takes pains to separate his own actions and experiences from those of Yehoshua.

1. Verse 6: *Concerning me and concerning you.* Reference is to BeMidbar 14:30, where the Ribbono shel Olam announces that Yehoshua and Kaleiv are to be exempted from the decree that this whole generation will die in the wilderness (Metzudos). The language that the Ribbono shel Olam uses clearly brackets them together: *except for Kaleiv ben Yefunneh and Yehoshua bin Nun.* So here, why not say *concerning us?*

2. Verse 7: Kaleiv delivered a report *expressing what was in my heart.* Both Rashi and Radak explain this phrase as follows: During the forty days of their assignment, Kaleiv did not allow the other spies to see that he was in opposition to them. He spoke as they did, so that they never suspected he would later turn against them. He sheltered his true feelings in his heart. There is no indication that Yehoshua did the same. As far as any available text is concerned, it is possible that Yehoshua never bothered to hide his feelings.

3. Verse 8: The most striking of all is Kaleiv's description of the spies as *my brothers.* In using this expression in talking to Yehoshua, he is clearly indicating that the ten spies were *his* brothers but not Yehoshua's. How were these dreadful sinners his "brothers"? If they were, why were they not also Yehoshua's?

The key to understanding probably lies in Sotah 34b, which tells how Kaleiv made his way to Chevron in order to pray for help. The language is as follows:

ויבאו מבעי ליה! אמר רבא: מלמד, שפירש כלב מעצת מרגלים והלך ונשתטח על קברי אבות, אמר להן: אבותי, בקשו עלי רחמים שאנצל מעצת מרגלים.

Why does the verse tell us that *he came* to Chevron? Should it not say that *they came*? Rava answered, "The singular form is used to tell us that only one of the spies, Kaleiv, went to Chevron. He distanced himself from the spies' plot and went to prostrate himself upon the graves of the patriarchs, saying, 'O my fathers! Please pray to the Ribbono shel Olam that He should have mercy upon me, that I might be saved from joining the spies' plot.'"

The language that Rava uses—*He distanced himself . . . and went*—implies that it was at that moment that Kaleiv distanced himself from the others. The inference is that when the spies originally set out, Kaleiv was of one mind with them. This would certainly put him into a category quite different from that of Yehoshua. Moshe Rabbeinu had prayed for Yehoshua and from that moment onwards, Yehoshua had nothing to do with the others. But Kaleiv had been one of the crowd, yet he had had the courage to change in midstream. That is a different story altogether.

We will offer a short summary of how these assumptions will answer the questions that we raised above. However, we will leave a fuller analysis to the next chapter.

1. It is a little early to deal with this anomaly in any detail. We would first need to know the material that is to be discussed in the following few chapters. For the moment, it is sufficient to point to two very different

17. Kaleiv I

futures that awaited Yehoshua and Kaleiv. Yehoshua is to succeed Moshe Rabbeinu and to bring Klal Yisrael into Eretz Yisrael. Kaleiv, through his marriage to Moshe Rabbeinu's sister, Miriam, will become the progenitor of David HaMelech and, through him, of the Mashiach. It is in order to meet these differing destinies that they were kept alive. The unexpected *concerning me and concerning you* turns out to be the logical formulation.

2. Yehoshua could never have hidden his intentions as did Kaleiv. From the beginning, it was clear to everybody that he stood aloof and had no common language with the other spies. It was only Kaleiv, who had in all seriousness been their collaborator, who was able to pull off this strategy.

3. Kaleiv, who had originally thought as they did, was able to look at the other spies as "brothers"; Yehoshua could not.

In the next chapter, we will begin to flesh out these theories. We will have to make some detours but, in the end, all the circular paths that we follow will converge and lead straight to our Messianic redemption.

18.

Kaleiv II

We have set ourselves a major task for this chapter. In the previous essay, we propounded a radical theory: that Kaleiv, in contrast to Yehoshua, had to struggle mightily to maintain his integrity. When he started out, he was strongly inclined to throw in his lot with the other spies. I cannot and do not expect you, dear reader, to accept this assertion without some solid documentation. I will provide that now.

I will go even further. I will argue that Kaleiv's original ambivalence was no accident. It was absolutely necessary that matters should develop as they did. I will suggest that it was specifically in order to ensure that Kaleiv would need to tilt against his own demons that Moshe Rabbeinu did not pray for Kaleiv as he had done for Yehoshua. He wanted Kaleiv to forge his own salvation. The story demanded it. More—as we shall see— Jewish history demanded it.

Let us tread carefully. We are approaching holy ground.

The Torah does not tell us much about Kaleiv. We know him only from his part in the saga of the spies.

18. Kaleiv II

There he appears as very much a two-dimensional figure: he was good where the others were bad, honest
where the others deceived, trusting where the others
trembled. Still, he remains a stranger to us. We know
of no pattern in his life that would explain why he alone,
among the eleven who had not been blessed, maintained
his integrity.

Yehoshua is different. We feel that we understand
him. As he is Moshe Rabbeinu's disciple, fortified by
Moshe Rabbeinu's prayers, we expect him to perform as
he should. We cannot say the same about Kaleiv. He is
just one name among eleven others. Nothing prepares us
for what is about to happen. There is no hint that he will
break out of the crowd.

So we are left guessing. Why was this man different
from all the others? From where *did* he draw his moral
resilience? He remains a question mark suspended in an
enigmatic "present." There is no past and there is no future. He appears to us as a stick figure with whom we can
do nothing useful.

In order to help us, the world of Aggadah beckons. It is
lavish where the written word is sparse. It provides a can-
vas covered in rich and vivid colors. Its hero is not just an
individual who rises to a difficult challenge but a linchpin
playing out its part at the very center of Jewish history.
In its hands, Kaleiv, seed of the kingly line of Yehudah,
becomes Kaleiv, progenitor of David HaMelech and,
through him, of the Mashiach.

We can find most of the material in Sotah 12a. The secrets that this passage unravels are locked into the text of
the first few chapters of I Divrey HaYamim.

Here are the points that are significant for our discussion. We will first trace each of them to the source from
which our Sages derive them and then attempt to draw
some conclusions.

1. Kaleiv married Moshe Rabbeinu's sister, Miriam.
2. David HaMelech was descended from that union.
3. Miriam had been a pale, sickly woman from whom all eligible suitors shied away. Only Kaleiv was willing to take her as his wife. With loving, fatherlike devotion, he nursed her back to health and youth.[1]
4. Kaleiv's willingness to marry a woman whom everybody else shunned is traced back to his determination to remain untouched by the spies' perfidy.

Here are the hints that our Sages find in Divrey HaYamim for these assertions. I will present only the bare facts. For a much fuller discussion, you might want to consult my ArtScroll commentary on Divrey HaYamim. The relevant verses are in chapters 2 and 4 of I Divrey HaYamim. I provide a wider discussion in Section Two, p. 388.

1. *Kaleiv took Efras as his wife* (2:19). Sotah 11b teaches that this was Miriam.[2]
2. David is described as an *Efrati* in I Shmuel 17:12.[3] This description marks him as a descendant of Miriam (see 1, above). See Rashi, Shemos 1:21.
3. *And Kaleiv ben Chetzron[4] fathered Azuvah and Yerios* (2:18). The two names, Azuvah and Yerios, are said to refer to Miriam. She was called Azuvah (*forsaken*) because no man wanted to marry her. She was called Yerios (*sheets*) because she was as white as a sheet. Kaleiv did not permit these disabilities to deter him. He married her and, as noted above, nursed her back to health and youth.
4. Throughout these passages dealing with Kaleiv's marriage to Miriam, he is assigned many different names. Almost all of these describe his stand in the matter of the spies. For our purpose, the most significant of these is Ashchur (*black*) because his face became black from hunger. He fasted constantly to elicit God's help

so as not to be caught up in the wiles of the spies. I regard this as particularly significant because it affirms my thesis that Kaleiv had been much inclined to follow the spies' lead.[5]

We have a lot of material here and we will be using all of it. Before we start our more general analysis, we should spend a few more moments on section 3. Miriam had been an invalid. Everyone was repelled by her sickly appearance. But Kaleiv saw what others failed to see. Beneath the ravages of a seemingly intractable disease, he knew that there lay a truer truth. His was a sharper vision than that of others. He did not permit the accidental to warp his perception of the essential. He was a man who could be trusted to have a true grasp of history.

Here is the passage from Sotah, which we simply must see before we continue.

ולאשחור אבי תקוע היו שתי נשים חלאה ונערה, אשחור זה כלב,
ולמה נקרא שמו אשחור, שהושחרו פניו בתעניות, אבי שנעשה לה
כאב, תקוע שתקע את לבו לאביו שבשמים. היו שתי נשים נעשה
מרים כשתי נשים, חלאה ונערה לא חלאה ונערה הואי, אלא בתחילה
חלאה ולבסוף נערה. ובני חלאה צרת וצחר ואתנן, צרת שנעשית צרה
לחברותיה, צחר שהיו פניה דומין כצהרים, אתנן שכל הרואה אותה
מוליך אתנן לאשתו.

Ashchur Avi Teko'a had two wives, Chel'ah and Na'arah.
"Ashchur" refers to Kaleiv ... because his face became blackened as a result of his fasting. "Avi" (*father*) hints at the fact that he behaved towards the ailing Miriam as though he were her father. "Teko'a" (*clinging*) hints at the fact that he fastened his heart to his Heavenly Father, thereby refusing to bow to the pressure of the spies.

Had two wives. Miriam went through a change that made her appear as though she were two separate wives .... At first she was ill (*Chel'ah*) and then she reverted to young girlhood (*Na'arah*).

Now the children of Chel'ah were Tzeres, Tzochar and Esnan. "Tzeres" (*plague*) hints at the fact that she made all other women suffer. She was so beautiful that husbands became less satisfied with their wives. "Tzochar" (*shining*) hints at the fact that her face shone like the midday sun. "Esnan" (*gift*) hints at the fact that any man who saw her beauty would immediately be moved to send his wife a present so that she would consent to be intimate with him.

Quite clearly, it is as we have said. The two stories in which Kaleiv is the hero—first, his refusal to bow to the blandishments of the spies, and second, his wisdom in seeing the sickly Miriam not as she was but as what she could become after receiving fatherly care—are one and the same. Both are energized by his unerring sense of what is essence and what accident. In both cases, his refusal to be deflected by surface appearances, his insistence on seeing the smile beneath the frown, won the day.

We are edging towards getting to know the Kaleiv who was destined to become the progenitor of the Mashiach. Let us savor our discoveries slowly and appreciatively. For this, we need another chapter.

19.

Kaleiv III

At the end of the previous chapter, we indicated that we were about ready to examine the significance of Kaleiv as the progenitor of the Mashiach. We are almost there, but not quite. In this chapter, we will make a final detour.

Let us listen to Yehoshua and Kaleiv in their initial reaction to the spies' negative report.

ו. ויהושע בן נון וכלב בן יפנה מן התרים את הארץ קרעו בגדיהם.

ז. ויאמרו אל כל עדת בני ישראל לאמר הארץ אשר עברנו בה לתור אתה טובה הארץ מאד מאד.

ח. אם חפץ בנו ידוד והביא אתנו אל הארץ הזאת ונתנה לנו ארץ אשר הוא זבת חלב ודבש.

ט. אך בידוד אל תמרדו ואתם אל תיראו את עם הארץ כי לחמנו הם סר צלם מעליהם וידוד אתנו אל תיראם.

6. Yehoshua bin Nun and Kaleiv ben Yefunneh, who had been among those who spied out the land, tore their clothes.

7. ...

8. ...

9. "Only do not rebel against God and, moreover, do not fear the inhabitants of the land, for they are *our food*.

139

Their *protective cloud* has moved away from them and God is with us. Do not be afraid of them."

Two expressions in verse 9 require our attention. Yehoshua and Kaleiv wanted to assure the people that they would have no trouble dealing with the inhabitants of the land. Why *our food*? Nowhere else in TaNaCh, as far as I have been able to discover, is "bread" used as a metaphor to describe people who are easy to vanquish. Also, *their protective cloud* needs thought. What cloud had protected them until now, and why had it now moved away, leaving them vulnerable?

First, then, *protective cloud*.

Rashi offers two explanations, of which the second reads, *the shade that the Ribbono shel Olam had spread over them has departed*. Why had God spread a protective cloud over the Canaanites, and why did it disappear now?

I believe that the answers lie in the truths that we discovered in Chapter 9. Here is what we wrote there:

> The Ribbono shel Olam's disposition that the land which He intended to give to His children should first fall to the descendants of Canaan was motivated by Canaan's status as slave to Shem. In this way Canaan would build up the land, till its fields and build its cities, in order that Avraham's children would find their possessions ready and developed for them when the time would come for them to take possession.
>
> This truth underlies the Ribbono shel Olam's promise that no weapons would be required for the Israelites to enter the land. Since they were the rightful owners, there was no historical imperative which would make a war necessary.

The Ribbono shel Olam would surely have wanted to protect the Canaanites in Eretz Yisrael as long as their task remained incomplete. However, once Klal Yisrael would be ready to enter the land, that protection would no longer be necessary. This is precisely what Yehoshua and Kaleiv were telling the people. Since it is now the Ribbono shel Olam's wish that we should enter the land, there is nothing that we have to fear from the Canaanites. The period of their indenture to us has ended. There is nothing to prevent us from merely walking in and taking our own.

This insight will also help us to understand the expression *our bread*. It is analogous to Koheles 5:8: *Earth is master of everybody; even a king is subordinate to the field.* The sense is that in our physical world we cannot get away from our physical needs. The mightiest kingdom can only be as strong as its agricultural base. Metzudos takes *the field* to mean *the farmer*, that is, *the man of the field. Even a king is subordinate to the farmer.* In the same way, we are able to take *our bread* as *the people who provide us with bread*. Yehoshua and Kaleiv are telling the people that the Canaanites had been given the land only in order to make it fertile for the Israelites. Because of this, the protection that they had enjoyed until now so that they could perform their task was no longer needed.

Read thus, the argument that Yehoshua and Kaleiv offered was really in support of God's assurance that the Israelites would not have to fight for the land. Yehoshua and Kaleiv were in effect saying that there was still time to disassociate completely from the spies. The whole idea of sending spies—that is, of opting for a military conquest of the land—had shown itself to be a bad idea. "Let us," Yehoshua and Kaleiv argued, "get back to the original plan. Let us trust in the Ribbono shel Olam rather than in our own prowess. All we have to do is to learn to think God's thoughts instead of our own."

I have the feeling that what we have now learned may help us deal with a textual oddity. As we know, Kaleiv was rewarded for his courageous stand against the spies by being granted Chevron and its environs as his ancestral home. We can understand that. He alone had had the courage to brave the giants who lived there, and it was appropriate that this be recognized. Nevertheless the language that the Torah uses here seems strange.

Here is Devarim 1:36: *I will give the land* UPON WHICH HE TROD *to him and his children, because he was loyal to the* Ribbono shel Olam. Why *upon which he trod*? In what way is his having "trodden" there a part of the logic? The same expression recurs in Yehoshua 14:9, making it obvious that somehow the "treading" is a significant part of the story. Here is the verse: *And Moshe swore on that day, saying: The land* UPON WHICH YOUR FOOT TROD *shall be your inheritance and for your children forever, for you were loyal to HaShem your God.*

I feel somewhat diffident about the solution that I am about to offer. None of the standard commentators seems to have thought along similar lines and, if it is to have any claim to be taken seriously, it will really need some firmer backing than I am able to offer. Nevertheless, after this *caveat emptor*, there seems to me no great harm in proposing what follows. It grows naturally out of the various truths that we have discovered in our series of essays. Moreover, the analysis of the relevant text that I am about to offer seems persuasive. I feel that what I have to say falls within the range of the possible.

Here is my idea. I base it upon the language used by Yehoshua and Kaleiv in their attempt to sway the people away from their calamitous intention to return to Egypt under new leadership. We will find confirmation of our thinking in Moshe Rabbeinu's address to the people in Devarim 1:30–33.

Here is the verse from Shlach (BeMidbar 14:8):

19. Kaleiv III

אם חפץ ה' בנו

והביא אתנו אל הארץ הזאת ונתנה לנו

ארץ אשר היא דבת חלב ודבש.

If HaShem wants us

He will bring us to this land and give it to us,

A land flowing with milk and honey.

Let us begin with the first phrase. We have translated it, *If HaShem wants us*. What exactly do we mean when we say the Ribbono shel Olam *wants* us? If we mean that He "loves" us, why not say so? We have phrases like *because HaShem has loved you* (Devarim 7:8) in the Torah, and we have a sense of what they mean. The fact is that nowhere else in the five books of the Torah does it say that the Ribbono shel Olam "wants" us or anybody else. Even in the rest of TaNaCh it occurs only very rarely.

There is another point. As we translated it, the phrase does not really make sense. We use the verb *to want* to describe an attitude towards something that we do not have but wish we did. We cannot use the word in relation to an object that we already own. I may love my car, I may be proud of it, but it would be meaningless to say that I "want" it. It is already mine, so there is nothing left to want. So what does our phrase really mean?

Moreover, the word for *us, banu,* really means *within us.* But the verb *wants* is transitive, and we would expect a direct object. Let us examine to what extent the idea of "wanting" anything is applicable to the Ribbono shel Olam, the Omnipotent.[1]

A good place to consider is BeMidbar Rabbah 10.

שוקיו עמודי שש וגו' שוקיו זה העולם שנשתוקק הקב"ה לבראתו כמה דתימא ועלי תשוקתו.

His thighs are pillars of marble (Shir HaShirim 5:15). [The description is a metaphor for God and] *shok,* His thighs, refers to *the world.* This because the Hebrew *shok* can

143

be derived from *shokek, to yearn.* The lesson is that God yearned to create this world, as is also expressed in *his yearning is centered upon me* (Shir HaShirim 7:11).

Apparently, there is one thing that even an omnipotent God lacks. He lacks the voluntary obeisance with which a creature full of love and awe turns to its creator. A cosmos infinitely full of infinite possibilities nevertheless lacks that one, vitally important, element. For that, God needs puny, fallible, imperfect man. There is no way around that. God longs for man because only man can provide the one thing that omnipotence cannot deliver.

Our wholehearted service, freely offered in love and submission, is the one thing—by definition the only thing—that the Ribbono shel Olam can "want" from us. Without us, He cannot have it.

I believe that we have found the correct translation of *If HaShem wants that which is "within us."* Meaning: *If* WITHIN *our community, as we stand here today, the Ribbono shel Olam can find the love and submission that He craves, then....*

Then what? We will find the answer in the second phrase, *He will* BRING *us to this land and* GIVE *it to us.* I believe that the key to understanding lies in the combination of the two words, *bring* and *give.* At this point, dear reader, I ask you to go back to Chapter 5 and to study with particular care the chart in which I contrast the VaEira passage with Shlach and Devarim. You will see that only in VaEira do we have both *bring* and *give.* In Shlach we have *bring*, but instead of *give* we have *know the land.* And in Devarim, although we have *give*, we do not have *bring* but rather *come.*

The conclusions that we reached in Chapter 5 were as follows. The original VaEira promise that HaShem would *bring* us into the land and *give* it to us was never fulfilled. It presupposed a nonmilitary mode of entry into the land: a process of being *brought* into the land and

19. Kaleiv III

taking possession by divine fiat as rightful owners, following which God would then *give* us the land in perpetuity.

Shlach does talk of our being *brought* into the land, but the implication is attenuated by the verse saying that we would only *know* the land, rather than that HaShem would *give* it to us. As Ramban reads it, *knowing* only describes a temporary stay to get to know the land, and that is all. In Devarim, HaShem does promise to *give* us the land, but the implication is attenuated by the phrase that we would *come* there, rather than being *brought*. The Jews would come under their own steam—not, as it were, upon the wings of the Ribbono shel Olam's eagles.

In both cases, the missing element shades the meaning of the word that is used. And so the *being brought* in Shlach is downgraded to less than the *being brought* in VaEira. Similarly, the *giving* of Devarim means less than the *giving* in VaEira.

But Yehoshua and Kaleiv brook no erosion of the original pronouncement's luster. They require only *if HaShem wants that which is within us*: if we can embody God's dreams, we can yet scale the heights that had once beckoned. The past, the promise that Hashem will both *bring* us into the land and *give* it to us, can be recovered. The error that we made in insisting that spies be sent need change nothing if we make sure that we, ourselves, do not change.

Yehoshua and Kaleiv were, in effect, saying that our free fall into smallness (see Chapter 9) could yet be reversed.

Yehoshua and Kaleiv—the one because of Moshe Rabbeinu's prayer, the other because of his own determination to stand straight—remained citizens of an earlier and better world.

It seems to me that this approach finds support in Moshe Rabbeinu's own words, as reported in Devarim 1:

כט. ואמר אלכם לא תערצון ולא תיראון מהם.

ל. ידוד אלהיכם ההלך לפניכם הוא ילחם לכם ככל אשר עשה אתכם במצרים לעיניכם.

לא. ובמדבר אשר ראית אשר נשאך ידוד אלהיך כאשר ישא איש את בנו בכל הדרך אשר הלכתם עד באכם עד המקום הזה.

לב. ובדבר הזה אינכם מאמינם בידוד אלהיכם.

לג. ההלך לפניכם בדרך לתור לכם מקום לחנתכם באש לילה לראתכם בדרך אשר תלכו בה ובענן יומם.

29. I said to you, "Do not allow your spirits to be broken. Do not fear the Canaanites.

30. "HaShem your God, Who has led you all along, He will be the one Who does battle for you in precisely the way that He helped you in Egypt, as you yourselves saw.

31. "Furthermore, you recall how, in the wilderness, He carried you just as a father would carry his son. . . .

32. "In spite of this you still did not believe in Hashem your God."

33. "[He is the God] Who leads you and finds the ideal place for you to camp. He provides a fiery pillar at night so that you can see your way, and a pillar of cloud by day."

Although the entire passage is germane to our discussion, verse 30 is particularly important for us. God will do battle for us as He did in Egypt. Now, in Egypt there was certainly no human involvement in the Ribbono shel Olam's battle against the Egyptians. In fact, no battle, as the word is normally understood, took place there at all. Still, God's help to us in Egypt is the paradigm for His helping us upon our entry into the land of Canaan. Clearly, a miraculous entry is contemplated. This is made evident throughout the passage we have quoted. Every one of the examples refers to a miraculous intervention on the part of the Ribbono shel Olam, without any human involvement at all.

Let us sum up. Even though, as we worked out in

Chapter 9, the people's request to send spies signaled a precipitous drop in their spiritual level, its effects, even at this late stage, were still reversible. Had Yehoshua and Kaleiv prevailed in their arguments, the entire sorry incident would have been neutralized and forgotten without leaving any mark.

That established, it seems clear that Kaleiv, from the moment that he went to Chevron—that is, from the moment that he decided to break ranks with the spies—was operating in the original mode. He was given Chevron, the place upon which his feet had *trodden*, because in that mode the promise that the Jews would acquire the land without military conquest still held good. In precisely the same way that Avraham had acquired the land by walking through it,[2] Kaleiv acquired Chevron by going there. The fact that later on he had to fight in order to dislodge those who had made their home in Chevron does not in any way disprove our contention. These people were squatters on *his* land and needed to be removed.

The time has come to open a new chapter, this one dedicated to examining the Kaleiv whom our Sages have introduced as progenitor of the Mashiach.

20.

Kaleiv IV

This morning I gave a class to a group of college students who were receiving their first exposure to Yiddishkeit. Predictably, they were interested in the concept of Israel as God's Chosen People. In the course of the discussion, I heard myself saying that, whatever else was implied, one aspect of that special relationship was certainly that we, as individuals and as a nation, were expected to serve as role models to the rest of mankind. If someone meets a Jew, he should know at once that here is an example of humanity at its noblest; if he observes us on the national level, he should feel that this is a community of which he would love to be a part.

As I was talking, I suddenly felt myself blushing. Would these young men, could these young men, take me seriously? They have only to turn on their television sets or to open their papers to meet Israel as a pariah state, the Jew as rapacious colonist, oppressor and killer of innocents. Whatever positive image we have of ourselves, the nations of the world certainly do not share it. Israel's flag fluttering bravely at the UN taunts us with our impotence. I suppose that Yirmeyahu's lament (Eichah

1:1), *How* ALONE *Yerushalayim dwells*, is a play on the Torah's *Behold, you shall be a nation dwelling* ALONE (BeMidbar 23:9). "Look," Yirmeyahu seems to be saying, "Look what you could have had and look once more, look well, where you have ended up." He could certainly have had our generation in mind. The United Nations are indeed united—in wishing heartily that we would all just disappear.

All this gave me much to think about, and I still had it on my mind when, later in the day, I sat down to begin work on the present chapter. I had promised that this would be the essay in which we would explore the significance of Kaleiv as the progenitor of the Mashiach. "Well," I thought, "how do this morning's observations comport with what we know about how Klal Yisrael will look in the time immediately preceding the advent of the Mashiach?"

My thoughts went to Yeshayahu 53 and 54, and I saw confirmation staring me in the face.

In the following chart, I examine four of the relevant verses from these two chapters. Taken together, they convey the gist of the entire section. The first is taken from chapter 52, the others from chapter 53. As Rashi reads them, they portray the shock that the nations feel when, after the Mashiach has come, they see the nation that they had always despised and vilified, which had always seemed so revolting, flowering into a thing of sublime beauty. Their shock turns into horror as the truth penetrates their hate-sodden minds. Their windows had been mirrors; what they had seen was their own leering grimace superimposed upon the refined features of the Jews.[1]

Here are the verses.

רש"י	ישעיהו נב ונג
הנה באחרית הימים יצליח עבדי יעקב צדיקים שבו.	יג. הנה ישכיל עבדי ירום ונשא וגבה מאד
מי האמין לשמועתינו, כן יאמרו העכו"ם איש לרעהו אילו היינו שומעים מפי אחרים מה שאנו רואים אין להאמין. וזרוע ה', כזאת בגדולה והוד על מי נגלת' עד הנה.	א. מי האמין לשמעתנו וזרוע ידוד על מי נגלתה.
היה	ג. נבזה וחדל אישים איש מכאבות וידוע חלי וכמסתר פנים ממנו נבזה ולא חשבנהו.
אכן חליינו הוא נשא, אכן ל' אבל בכל מקום אבל עתה אנו רואים שלא מחמ' שפלותו בא לו אלא מיוסר היה ביסורין. ואנחנו חשבנוהו, אנו היינו סבורים שהוא שנאוי למקום והוא לא היה כן. . . .	ד. אכן חלינו הוא נשא ומכאבינו סבלם ואנחנו חשבנהו נגוע מכה אלהים ומענה.

Here is the chart in translation:[2]

YESHAYAHU 52, 53	RASHI
13. Indeed, My servant will prosper, be exalted and raised to great heights.	As history will have run its course, My servant Ya'akov, that is, those who maintained their righteousness, will be vindicated.

1. Who would ever have believed this! ...	The nations will say to one another, "Had we not seen this with our very own eyes, we would never have believed it."
3. He was always so despised, appeared to be hardly human. Racked by pain, familiar with disease. We could not bear to look at him. He was despicable, we held him of no account.	This is a description of what used to be in the past.
4. Yet he was smitten by *our* sickness. He was enduring *our* pain. We accounted him plagued, smitten and afflicted by God.	We now realize that his revolting appearance came about only because of his intense suffering. This came about not, as we had thought, because he was hated by God. That was not at all the case. He had been sickened because of *our* sins. His suffering was the result of *our* rebellions. [He was simply a reflection of what we ourselves were.]

Quite clearly, it is to be the Mashiach's task to reveal the essential health of a sorely afflicted people. He will find us in many ways unattractive. Two thousand years of exile have left us deeply scarred. He will, as did Shlomo HaMelech before him, understand that:

ה. שחורה אני ונאוה בנות ירושלם כאהלי קדר כיריעות שלמה.
ו. אל תראוני שאני שחרחרת ששזפתני השמש . . .

5. Even though I am black, I am pleasing, O daughters
of Yerushalayim. Though I appear as black as the tents
of Arabia, I can readily become [as dazzling white] as
the curtains of Shlomo.

6. Do not look down upon me because of my swarthy
skin. It is so only because the sun has gazed down upon
me. . . .

Here is what Rashi has to say on these two verses.

. . . אל אקל בעיניכם אף אם עזבני אישי מפני שחרות שבי . . . לפי שאין
שחרותי וכיעורי ממעי אמי אלא על ידי שזיפת השמש שאותו שחרות
נוח להתלבן כשיעמוד בצל.

Do not scorn me, although my husband has left me
because of my swarthy features . . . I was not born dark-
skinned but became so only because the sun was allowed
to burn down upon me. Such swarthiness is easily corrected, by moving into the shade.

We are all fully aware of our sometimes unpleasant
appearance. Still, we know that it is aberrant. It is not reflective of our true selves. Let us only move out of reach
of the burning sun of exile, let us enter the shade of the
Almighty—*sitting in the shelter of the Supernal One, dwelling
in the shadow of the Almighty One* (Tehillim 91:1)—and we
will very quickly rediscover our true selves.

The task that we set ourselves for this essay was to
probe the significance of David HaMelech's, and therefore the Mashiach's, descent from Kaleiv. If we recall
what we have learned in the last few chapters, the truth
will jump out at us. We recognized that Kaleiv's ability
to see the true Miriam beneath the sickly, unwholesome
exterior was of a piece with his ability to see the real Eretz

Yisrael beneath the inhospitable exterior that misled the other spies. We now know that it is precisely this ability that defines the function of the Mashiach. Substitute repellent Klal Yisrael in its exilic guise for the ugly Miriam whom nobody wanted, and we have the Kaleiv whom we have come to know in a new incarnation, riding to the rescue.

The time has come to reread Chapter 15. There we suggested that it makes sense to anticipate that the remedy for the wound inflicted by the spies should come from within their own ranks. We have now made the case for this assumption. The spies, as we have demonstrated, radically changed the course of Jewish history. It will not, it cannot, be righted until the advent of the Mashiach. Kaleiv, very much one of the spies, unfortified by any intercession by Moshe Rabbeinu, struggled mightily to retain his Jewish integrity. In the short run, the other ten spies can be viewed as the victors in this tragic confrontation. Those who had left Egypt were condemned to die in the wilderness. But in the long run, Kaleiv won out. By his heroic refusal to take the easy path, he laid the groundwork for the Mashiach and the final redemption.

21.

When Leopards Change Their Spots

I have come to the end of this book of tear-drenched nights. The "nights," of course, refer to the millennia of iterations of Tish'ah BeAv. Fortunate is the man or woman who can shed hot tears of sorrow and longing amid the darkness of exile that envelops us on that bleak and desolate day.

And now, before we part ways at the end of the long and complicated journey that you and I have traveled together, I want to examine the idea of *tears* a little more closely. We have all cried—sometimes from joy, more often from sorrow. Have you ever wondered, as I have done many times, why we express both emotions in the same way? Why was the Ribbono shel Olam, usually so generous with the wondrous resources with which He has endowed us, so parsimonious in this respect? Was there not some way to differentiate more clearly between joy and sorrow?

On a physiological level, my encyclopedia informs me, "strong emotion causes the tear ducts to constrict and to emit tears." That, at least, takes care of the technicalities. It seems logical enough that strong emotions should cause constriction, which sets the process of crying

21. When Leopards Change Their Spots

in motion, and one cannot complain if the tear ducts are unable or unwilling to differentiate between sorrow and joy. If understanding physiology were our goal, we could stop right here. However, because it is not, let us delve below the surface in order to understand why it all works as it does.

Perhaps the best place to begin is Zechariah 8:19:

כה אמר ידוד צבאות צום הרביעי וצום החמישי וצום השביעי וצום
העשירי יהיה לבית יהודה לששון ולשמחה ולמעדים טובים והאמת
והשלום אהבו.

Thus speaks the Lord of Hosts: "The fast of the fourth month [Shiv'ah Asar B'Tamuz] and the fast of the fifth month [Tish'ah B'Av] and the fast of the seventh month [Tzom Gedaliah] and the fast of the tenth month [Asarah B'Teives] will [one day] turn into days of joy and celebration for the family of Yehudah, provided only that the [people] will learn to love truth and peace."

It is understandable enough that, once Mashiach comes and the Beis HaMikdash is rebuilt, the fast days on which we now commemorate the tragedies that attended the destruction of the first Beis HaMikdash will lose their relevance. Had the prophet simply said that the time will come when the mourning associated with these days will be abrogated, we would have understood him perfectly. But he says more than that. The sorrow that we now feel on those days[1] will not simply vanish but will reappear in the form of joy and celebration. The fast days will be transformed into festivals. This is certainly far more than we would have expected.

The theme that sorrow will one day not only give way to joy but actually turn into joy seems to be a staple of Jewish historiography.

A particularly graphic example of this appears in Yirmeyahu 31:12. First, however—if we are to appreciate the full significance of this passage—we will need a little

155

background. Yirmeyahu knew a thing or two about the dreadful pain of loss and rejection. In Bava Basra (14b), our Sages describe his book of prophecy (in contrast to those of Yechezkel and Yeshayahu) as being devoted entirely to the theme of destruction. Yet even a cursory reading yields many passages that speak of the ultimate redemption in the most sublime terms. One of these is Chapter 31, of which we will quote just three verses.

יא. ובאו ורננו במרום ציון ונהרו אל טוב ידוד על דגן ועל תירש ועל יצהר ועל בני צאן ובקר והיתה נפשם כגן רוה ולא יוסיפו לדאבה עוד.

יב. אז תשמח בתולה במחול ובחרים וזקנים יחדו והפכתי אבלם לששון ונחמתים ושמחתים מיגונם.

יג. ורויתי נפש הכהנים דשן ועמי את טובי ישבעו נאם ידוד.

11. They shall come and jubilate on Zion's heights, making their way towards God's bounty [of] new grain, wine and oil, sheep and cattle. They shall flourish like a watered garden, never again to give way to sorrow.

12. Then the young women will dance gaily, young men and elders together. I will turn their mourning to joy. I will comfort them and cheer them in their grief.

13. I will give their Kohanim their fill of fatness, and My people will enjoy My full bounty.[2]

There is not much mention of "destruction" here, is there? Or maybe, just maybe, there is. In the context of our discussion, it should be clear that our main focus is on the expression in verse 12: "I will turn their mourning to joy." This phrase echoes clearly the thesis that we saw expressed by Zechariah. Yirmeyahu is not predicting some new joyous celebration with no roots in the past. Rather, God will turn the mourning of centuries into joy.

That just Yirmeyahu, of all the prophets, should have spoken of such a metamorphosis is of particular significance, because it seems to stand in contradiction to another of his prophecies. Once more we will quote three

21. When Leopards Change Their Spots

verses—these with a very different message. They come from 13:22–24.

כב. וכי תאמרי בלבבך מדוע קראני אלה ברב עונך נגלו שוליך נחמסו עקביך.

כג. היהפך כושי עורו ונמר חברברתיו גם אתם תוכלו להיטיב למדי הרע.

כד. ואפיצם כקש עובר לרוח מדבר.

22. When you ask yourself, "Why have these things befallen me?" it is because your skirts are lifted up, your ankles are revealed.[3]

23. Can the Ethiopian change his skin, or the leopard his spots? No more can you, so practiced in evil, change your ways.

24. So I will scatter you like straw that flies before the desert winds.

I feel that Yirmeyahu 13:23—"Can the Ethiopian change his skin?"—must be read in conjunction with 31:12, "I will turn their mourning into joy." The same Yirmeyahu who in Chapter 13 is utterly convinced that things have simply gone too far and that no change can be anticipated turns around completely in Chapter 31, for there we learn that the very days on which we had always commemorated our tragic experiences will themselves become days of unbounded joy.

At this point, we have supplied the interpretation to the strange title of this essay—yes, leopards can change their spots. But more than that, we have been empowered to suggest a reasonable answer to the puzzling statement in Bava Basra 14b that Yirmeyahu deals only with destruction—puzzling because clearly there are sections that paint the ultimate redemption in the most magnificent colors.

The answer would now seem self-evident. Yirmeyahu's vision of the future in Chapter 31 is grounded in the past. That vision is simply the result of viewing the destruction that otherwise occupies him throughout his prophecies from a different perspective. The sublime descriptions tell us how that destruction will look from the viewpoint of the Messianic era.

I do not feel equal to the task of writing what needs to be expressed. That demands a more penetrating depth than any that I have plumbed, a more profound understanding of God's ways than has been granted me to apprehend. It certainly requires a more eloquent voice— which really means a more eloquent heart—than mine. What we have here discovered continues the theme that we touched upon in the prologue to this book—which can, I suppose, be summed up in R. Akiva's famous dictum, "Anything at all which the Ribbono shel Olam does is ultimately for the good." In the long view of the Torah, no tragedy is completely tragic, no sorrow is so dark but that light lies right beyond the horizon. There is no destruction but that it carries redemption on its wings.

Dear reader, you and I have met with much sadness in the pages of this book. As we get ready to part ways, let us conjure up a picture that we can take and carry with us wherever life will lead us.

Let us rewind the clock of history for just a moment and transport ourselves to that pregnant moment when Yosef, viceroy of imperial Egypt, revealed himself to his brothers. At first, Yosef addressed all of them equally with words of comfort, encouragement and promise. But eventually the moment came when he permitted his feelings to overwhelm him, and he and Binyamin fell upon each other's shoulders, weeping.

Why were they crying?

Rashi cites our Sages' teaching that each one cried in anticipation of the destruction that the other would experience.

21. When Leopards Change Their Spots

The Mishkan that had served the Jews until Shlomo
HaMelech built the Beis HaMikdash had been erected
in Shiloh, an area situated within Yosef's portion of Eretz
Yisrael. Binyamin cried because that Mishkan would one
day stand in ruins after the Philistines captured the Holy
Ark.

Shlomo HaMelech's Beis HaMikdash and the second
Beis HaMikdash built when the exiles returned from
Babylon stood largely in Binyamin's portion. Both of
them would be destroyed. And so Yosef wept in anticipation of those two tragedies.

As it stands, this teaching is difficult to understand.
Why would the two brothers choose just this happy moment to mourn tragedies that lay far in the future?

Because this question poses such a serious difficulty,
Maharal [See *Gur Aryeh* on BeReishis 45:14] re-inter-
prets our Sages' tradition. In his view, the reconciliation
between Yosef and his brothers presages the ultimate
reunion between the ten lost tribes (symbolized by
Yosef) and the truncated remnant of once-proud Judea
that remained after Assyria took the inhabitants of the
Northern Kingdom into captivity, and which, until
today, has borne the burden of Jewish history (repre-
sented by Yehudah).

That reunion, Maharal maintains, will be accompa-
nied by many tears. He cites Yirmeyahu 31:5–9, which
speaks of the return of the Ten Tribes:

ה. כי יש יום קראו נצרים בהר אפרים קומו ונעלה ציון אל ידוד
אלהינו.

ו. כי כה אמר ידוד רנו ליעקב שמחה וצהלו בראש הגוים השמיעו הללו
ואמרו הושע ידוד את עמך את שארית ישראל.

ז. הנני מביא אותם מארץ צפון וקבצתים מירכתי ארץ בם עור ופסח
הרה וילדת יחדו קהל גדול ישובו הנה.

ח. בבכי יבאו ובתחנונים אובילם אוליכם אל נחלי מים בדרך ישר לא
יכשלו בה כי הייתי לישראל לאב ואפרים בכרי הוא.

5. For the day is coming when watchmen will proclaim on the heights of Efraim, "Come, let us go up to Zion, to HaShem our God."

6. Thus says HaShem, "Cry out in joy for Ya'akov, shout at the crossroads of the nations, let all hear your praises and say, 'O HaShem, save Your people, the remnants of Israel!'

7. "See, I will bring them back from the north and I will gather them from the very ends of the earth, the blind and the lame among them, those with child and those who are birthing—in a vast throng they will return here.

8. "They shall come with weeping, and because of their prayers I will guide them, I will lead them to streams of water, by a level road where they will not stumble, for I have always been a father to Israel. Efraim is my very first-born."

Why will they be crying? Clearly, the tears of which Yirmeyahu speaks will be tears of joy, born of the realization that at long last the horrors of galus lie behind them.

Maharal words it as follows: "When Yehudah and Yosef finally meet, they will cry about the sorrows and destructions that have overtaken them." It is an interesting formulation. Their tears of joy will be for the sorrows and destructions that they have suffered. What can this possibly mean?

Surely Maharal's ideas confirm everything that we have suggested in this essay. The tears of sorrow that they had shed at the time of their dreadful suffering will turn into tears of joy once the exile will have run its course.

We began this essay by wondering why suffering and happiness should express themselves in identical ways. Why do both bring us to tears? We have now discovered that the technical explanation which we offered above expresses a much deeper reality. The troubles that overtake

21. When Leopards Change Their Spots

us bring us to tears when they strike us with their cruel immediacy, and *later* they bring us to tears when we finally grow free of them. It is all the one Hand of God. He strikes and He heals—He strikes in order that we may be healed. The sorrow is the mask; the rejoicing, the reality.

We have shed many tears. But those tears have not been lost. The time will come when they will return to us, and we will welcome them and lose ourselves in their warmth and care.

בבכי יבאו ובתחנונים אובילם

Appendix to
Chapter 3

Why did the Ribono shel Olam insist that only Moshe Rabbeinu set up the Mishkan as a whole? The Midrash that we cited ascribes this to the fact that Moshe had played no role in the construction of the Mishkan's individual components. This, of course, begs the question: Why hadn't Moshe made any effort to be involved in these preparatory stages?

Here is a suggestion. In a number of places, Ramban makes the point that "the inner meaning of the Mishkan is that it served as a perpetuation of the Sinai experience." Thus, for example, he maintains that the voice that communicated with Moshe Rabbeinu from atop the holy Ark was the same voice that had spoken to him at Sinai.

I would argue that this particular aspect of the Mishkan—its recreation of the Sinai experience—had ramifications solely for Moshe Rabbeinu. At Sinai, he alone had climbed the mountain, and in the Mishkan he alone was privy to God's word.

For everybody else, the Mishkan's functions were the more obvious ones—such as its being the prescribed location for the sacrificial service. In the context of those functions, the Jews could relate to the various components of the Mishkan as separate entities. For one example, we might turn to Bava Basra 25b: "He who would be wise, let him turn southwards [towards the Menorah]. He who would be rich, let him turn northwards [towards the Shulchan]. Or we could go to Makkos 12a, where we learn that under certain circumstances a murderer who ascends the altar may not be killed there.

However, only when taken as a whole does the Mishkan attain the characteristic of the Sinai experience.[1] Moshe Rabbeinu did not relate to the individual components of the Mishkan. That is because relating to the Mishkan as a conglomeration of parts would have betrayed his experience of it as a whole. Therefore, he sought no role in creating those parts. It was only when the entire edifice could be raised that he became involved.[2]

We can now understand why the Ribono shel Olam insisted that only Moshe Rabbeinu should raise the Mishkan. Because only he had been allowed to ascend the mountain, only he would be able to recreate the mountain in the construction of the Mishkan.

Appendix to
Chapter 6

In endnote 9 to Chapter 6, I discussed how it is that the phrase *I have forgiven according to your words* occupies such an important place in our Selichos prayers, even though—as is clear from both Rashi and Ramban—in context, it has a limiting rather than an expansive meaning.

Upon consideration, the following seems possible.

In his commentary on Shemos 29:45-46, Ramban asserts that the phrase *to dwell in their midst* implies that the Mishkan, in some way, fills the needs of the Ribono shel Olam. Ramban cites a number of verses which seem to confirm this. Among them is Yehoshua 7:9[1]: *And what will You do for the sake of Your great name?* In his edition of Ramban's commentary, R. Chavel quotes Abusaula, who comments on this verse, "That is to say: If our enemies eradicate our name, [they will also eradicate] Your name, which is greater than ours. And so *what will You do for the sake of Your great name?* If we are not here, then neither will [the Divine] 'I' be here."

This verse (together with the others which Ramban cites) indicates that the Mishkan is—however we are to understand this—"necessary for God." The Ribono shel Olam "needs" to dwell among us, as it were.

That given, we can understand *I have forgiven according to your words* as Rashi does, and yet still read it positively. God's forgiveness is based not upon Moshe's prayer but upon his assertion of the indivisible link between God and the Jewish people. The sense is not, in contrast to Ramban's assertion, that Moshe's prayers were impotent, but rather that they were not required. The unison between the Ribono shel Olam and the Jewish people is so strong that nothing else is required. It is as though the Ribono shel Olam is saying that He will forgive because he "needs" to forgive. Anything else, even prayer, is superfluous.

Perhaps the custom to make these verses central to our Selichos services is based upon this understanding.

Appendix to
Chapter 12

Our analysis of the impetus behind the episode of the Meraglim yielded the insight that the rebellion expressed a preference for the comfortable, undemanding commonplace over the daily challenge into the unknown and unknowable that the special relationship that the Ribono shel Olam was proposing to the Jews offered. It is not easy to bear the burdens of greatness, and that generation wanted none of it.

We can recognize a similar attitude governing the people's feelings towards the manna. Manna was no ordinary food, and the people who were privileged to be sustained by it could not be ordinary either. Our Sages say that it was a food "fit for angels," a reified expression of the radiance of God's Presence (Ramban). Clearly, it would make heavy demands upon their behavior. Angel food is not for everybody.

The Jews of the desert seem to have coped with the manna well enough most of the time. However, twice matters came to a boil and the Jews complained: once in the second year (B'ha'aloschah) and once in the fortieth

(Chukos). Yet neither episode seems to have occurred at a reasonable time.

In the B'ha'aloschah episode, the Jews were standing at the border of the Promised Land. Had they not grumbled (that is, had the episode of the quail not intervened, had Miriam and Aharon not slandered Moshe Rabbeinu, and had the people not decided that they wished to send Meraglim) the Jews would have entered the land of Israel immediately without any problems. Once there, the manna would presumably have come to an end. Could they not have borne the burden of eating the manna for a few more days?

The same question pertains to the episode in Chukos. It was the end of the forty year trek through the wilderness. All was ready for a triumphant entry into the land. For thirty-eight years of wandering through the inhospitable desert, the Jews had eaten the manna without any problems. There is no record that they had expressed any dissatisfaction. Now, with one foot almost upon the Promised Land, they began once more to grumble.

What are we to make of all this?

It is the story of the Meraglim all over again. It was one thing to live miraculously for a relatively short period in the wilderness—quite another to bring miraculous living home.

The Jews did not want to enter the land of Israel as consumers of manna. They dreamed of sitting *in the shade of [their] vines and fig trees*. At home they craved the peace and quiet of the unchallenged life.

Notes

Prologue: Some Ruminations About Our History

1. See Ravad's gloss to the Rambam cited here.

2. This essay is not the place to count up all causes for that depression. Suffice it to say that the picture of our precious Jews carousing in a drunken stupor at Achashveirosh's feast tells us of a terrible self-hatred and nihilism that must have taken hold of them. Let us remember also that they had recently, at enormous self-sacrifice, begun rebuilding the Beis HaMikdash, only to be frustrated by Achashveirosh's decree, which he issued upon ascending the throne. They must certainly have felt themselves rejected by the Ribbono shel Olam.

3. There is much discussion among the commentators concerning the phrase *the halachos of the oral Torah*. But this is a subject beyond the scope of the present essay.

4. Rambam's source appears to be the Yerushalmi, Megillah 1:5. Here is the passage:

ר' יוחנן ורבי שמעון בן לקיש רבי יוחנן אמר הנביאים והכתובים עתידין ליבטל וחמשת
סיפרי תורה אינן עתידין ליבטל מה טעמא קול גדול ולא יסף רבי שמעון בן לקיש אמר
אף מגילת אסתר והלכות אינן עתידין ליבטל נאמר כאן קול גדול ולא יסף ונאמר להלן
וזכרם לא יסוף מזרעם.

R. Yochanan speaks only of the five books of the Torah and does not mention the Book of Esther at all. Reish Lakish mentions the Book of Esther together with the halachos, but derives them from different verses. Neither of them in any way *compares* the Book of Esther's resilience to that of either the Torah or the halachos. Rambam does make that comparison.

5. The Gemara uses this insight as the basis for certain halachic issues concerning the way Megillas Esther is to be written. These halachic ramifications need not concern us here.

6. See *Chiddushei HaGriz* on *Hilchos Megillah* 2:9. See also HaRav Binyamin Palier, *zatzal*, in *Am HaTorah*, vol. 4, issue 11, 5764. The assertion that the Book of Esther actually has characteristics of

169

the Torah is based upon the homiletic teaching from the Talmud (Megillah 16b): WORDS OF PEACE AND TRUTH—*i.e., like the truth of the Torah.*

7. This is how commentators read *And No'ach found favor.*

8. The Holy One, blessed be He, said: "In this world, because of the evil inclination, mankind split into seventy nations. But in the world-to-come, all will be equal, and together will call on My name and serve Me."

9. I use the term "identified" advisedly. I understand that the Vilna Gaon points out that the first set of Tablets had the words engraved into them, while the second set of Tablets was not engraved but written upon. Words that are engraved become an integral part of the material, whereas the ink used in writing is never more than a separate entity. The Sages who made the connection between the words *charus*, engraved, and *cheirus*, free, were referring to the first set of Tablets. There would have been a total identification with the Torah, and that would have made us free. With the second set of Tablets, the formulation became *Only a person who toils in learning Torah is free.* Our toil still makes an identification possible.

10. We have assumed that the change from the first set to the second set of Tablets is to be regarded as a regression. In an objective sense, that is of course true. However, it is undoubtedly also true that all of us who are blessed with the ability to toil in learning Torah are grateful that we are blessed with a Torah for which we have to go through the sweet struggle of "learning." Thus, from our vantage point, the regression contains a strong progressive or positive element.

Introduction

1. I stress "each one of them" because the text of Tehillim 137 seems to yield this. It begins in the plural, על נהרות בבל שם ישבנו—*alongside the rivers of Babylon, there* WE *sat*—but continues in the singular, אם **אשכחך** ירושלם תשכח ימיני—*if* I *forget you, Yerushalayim, may* MY *right hand wither.*

2. Thus, Ibn Ezra.

3. The context, ... תדבק לשוני—*may my tongue cleave to my palate*—demands that זכר, usually translated as *remember,* here be taken as *mention.* We see the same use of the word in למען תזכור את יום צאתך מארץ מצרים—*that you may* MAKE MENTION OF *the day of your exodus from Egypt.*

4. The fast on the tenth day of Teves commemorates the siege that Nevuchadnetzar launched against Yerushalayim three years before the Destruction. The fast on the seventeenth of Tammuz recalls the breaching of Yerushalayim's walls. On Tish'ah B'Av, the saddest day of all, the Beis HaMikdash was destroyed. The Fast of

Gedaliah has its own tragic story. Gedaliah was the governor whom Nevuchadnetzar appointed over the poor remnant of the people left in the land after the main body of Klal Yisrael had been dragged into exile. His subsequent assassination triggered a series of events that eventually led to the precipitous flight of the last remaining Jews to Egypt, where they perished. With the end of that sad episode, the Jewish presence in the land came to an end.

5. The implications of Shlomo HaMelech's inauguration of the Beis HaMikdash went far beyond the building itself. For the first and last time in Jewish history (until the coming of the Mashiach), all the conditions for ideal Jewish settlement in Eretz Yisrael were in place. Prophets walked the land and the Kohen Gadol wore and was able to consult the Urim VeTumim. Because all Jews lived in the land, the Yovel (or Jubilee year) with all its attendant halachos could be celebrated. Above all, the Beis HaMikdash was now in place in Yerushalayim. In a sense, this moment could be viewed as the culmination of the Exodus from Egypt. All that God had then promised had now come about.

One would therefore certainly have thought that this event was of sufficient moment to warrant some form of notice in our calendar.

Chapter 1. Missed Opportunities

1. It is a complex story, and the commentators are not of one mind about the nature of David's transgression. Rashi believes that David ordered a census without requiring the half shekel that the Torah mandates. Others maintain that David insisted that everyone, even those who were not yet twenty years old, be counted. Then there are those who believe that the problem lay in David's motivation. The Torah permits counting the Jews only when required for specific and legitimate reasons. Here David simply wanted to take joy in the vast number of subjects over whom he ruled.

In my ArtScroll commentary on Divrey HaYamim, I attempt to analyze the various possibilities and to understand how David rationalized his actions to himself. There is much that can be said on these issues, but all this would lead us too far afield for the purposes of this essay. Here we are concerned specifically with Ramban's understanding of this astounding event.

2. ויאמר הנה אנכי חטאתי ואנכי העויתי ואלה הצאן מה עשו תהי נא ידך בי ובבית אבי (שמואל ב כד טז)—*He said, Behold, I sinned and I twisted matters,* BUT AS FOR THESE SHEEP, *what have they done? Send Your Hand against me and my father's house* (II Shmuel 24:16).

3. It would clearly be wrong for the people to be punished for David's transgression. Later in the story, David does say to the Ribbono shel Olam that he, the guilty party should be punished,

not the people, who had had no part in his decision. However, in the course of our discussion we will learn that the people were not as innocent as may be supposed.

4. The further I get into this chapter, the more I see how difficult it is to treat this episode with the bare-bones format that I am using. A thoroughgoing analysis of this episode is complicated by the fact that it is described twice in TaNaCh—once in II Shmuel and once in I Divrey HaYamim. Most of the differences between the two accounts are relatively minor and can be resolved readily enough. However, there is one difference that is very major indeed. The Shmuel account ends with the cessation of the plague. The story is self-contained. However, in Divrey HaYamim the episode is only a springboard for identifying the site upon which the Beis HaMikdash was to be built. There are then another eight chapters, completely missing from the Shmuel account, that describe the preparations which David HaMelech made for the moment when Shlomo would be finally able to build the Beis HaMikdash.

Another significant difference is in the introductory verse. The one which we quoted here is taken from the Shmuel account. The verse which introduces the Divrey HaYamim account is significantly different.

The reader who has kept up with this rather prolix presentation will by now have understood that in this essay I am guilty of mixing and matching. I am using Shmuel's introductory verse but basing my argument upon the Divrey HaYamim version, which sees the story as an introduction to the preparations that David undertook for the building of the Beis HaMikdash.

Of course this is not really a problem, since the two accounts are obviously not contradictory but complementary.

I am afraid that you, dear reader, may feel frustrated by my treatment of the story here. It is obviously extremely important, and one would want to investigate it more fully. However, that is not possible in the present context. I can only suggest that you might want to go to my commentary on Divrey HaYamim, where I offer a very full treatment.

Chapter 2. Another Miscalculation

1. Part of the problem lies in the fact that the plural of *olam* seems to be *olamos*, not *olamim* (see, for example, the Mishnah in Uktzin 3:2).

2. A habitation which is to continue to all eternity makes sense, even though the Beis HaMikdash was twice destroyed. Reference is not to the bricks and stones of the building but to the inherent sanctity

of the location. See Rambam, Beis HaBechirah 6:16: *the holiness of the Beis HaMikdash and Yerushalayim derive from God's Presence, and God's Presence is never absent.*

3. This is also how Metzudos explains the verse. It must, however, be noted that Radak understands *the Rock of* OLAMIM as *the Rock Who will protect him to all eternity.*

Perhaps, after all, the two meanings are not so very far apart. We have already noted in endnote 1 that the plural of *olam* is *olamos*, not *olamim*. *Olamim* is thus not the regular plural form but a noun that denotes a duality of worlds, worlds that at some level constitute a composite. (I owe some of this insight to HaRav Shimon Schwab, *zatzal*, in his commentary on the Siddur.) As a composite, the two worlds (space)—which, after all, span the entirety of time—are coextensive with eternity (time).

(It is interesting that the English *world* was also once used for both time and space. See *Studies in Words* by C. S. Lewis, Cambridge University Press 1967.)

Here is a question to ponder. The section of our morning prayers entitled *Pesukey DeZimra*, Verses of Praise, is bracketed between two blessings: *Baruch She'Amar* at the beginning and *Yishtabach* at the end. In *Baruch She'Amar*, we refer to the Ribbono shel Olam as *Unique One, the Life-Force of the Olamim*; in *Yishtabach*, the closing blessing, ends with the words *King, God, the Life-Force of the Olamim.* Why both before and after *Pesukey DeZimra* do we speak of God as the Life-Force of the *Olamim*?

Here is my suggestion, which I offer with a degree of diffidence. It really is no more than a suggestion.

We begin *Pesukey DeZimra* with a blessing in which we praise "the One Who spoke and Who, by means of this speech, brought the *olam* into being." Let us leave aside for the moment what exactly this *olam* might be. At this point, it is sufficient to note that, by the end of *Baruch She'Amar*, this *olam* has changed to *olamim*, as we recorded above. The explanation lies in a more thorough understanding of the entire passage.

HaRav Yitzchak Hutner, *zatzal*, mentions in one of his essays that the act of creation is so fraught with mystery that the opening blessing of *Baruch She'Amar*, which deals with the act of creation—*brought the olam into being*—is unique in the sense that it does not contain the word *Atah*, You. The familiarity implied by the use of the second person, difficult enough when applied to the Ribbono shel Olam Who *governs* the world, would be totally out of place when we speak of the Ribbono shel Olam *creating* the world. In that context, we know Him not at all.

But why speak of the Ribbono shel Olam as Creator at all? How is the act of creation significant in the context of our *Pesukey DeZimra*?

The *Pesukey DeZimra* is taken mainly from the Book of Tehillim. In his pioneering book, *David King of Israel*, Henry Bieberfeld makes a profound observation. In writing his Tehillim, David HaMelech chose to take many of his life's experiences as reflective of the deeper truths or paradigms which animated them. For example, David composed Psalm 52 in reaction to Do'eg HaEdomi's perfidy in revealing David's hiding place to Sha'ul. However, instead of describing that incident as it happened, David writes a meditation on evil in the most general terms. Do'eg the man fades into Do'eg the idea. The thoughtful reader will find the same method at work throughout the book.

Pesukey DeZimra consists principally of descriptions of the power and beauty of nature. Tehillim 29:7, Kol HaShem BaKo'ach, Kol HaShem BeHadar, can be translated as *Both the titanic forces that rule our world and the breathtaking beauty that adorns it are simply God's voice penetrating to us.* The will of the Ribbono shel Olam resides within all that we can see, touch or experience. All these hide more than they reveal. A tree is no more than a representation of the paradigm or idea "tree," a clap of thunder is nothing but an echo of the titanic forces and might that fill the universe.

I believe that this is an aspect of the mystery of creation, which, in Rav Hutner's view, made the use of *You* in *Baruch She'Amar* inappropriate. But when the Ribbono shel Olam was in the act of creating the world, He was primarily busy with the "idea." The individual object evolved from this "idea" but is not coextensive with it. And since we humans experience only the object, never the "idea," we cannot address the Ribbono shel Olam engaged in creation with the familiar second person.

However, once the world exists and we observe it through individual objects, there is nothing to prevent us from understanding it intelligibly, though not experientially, as having a dual nature. It is therefore appropriate that *Pesukey DeZimra*, the chapters of Tehillim that celebrate the inner as well as the outer world, should be bracketed between two blessings that celebrate the Ribbono shel Olam as *the Life-Force of the Olamim.*

If in all these conjectures we have come close to some kind of truth, then the change from *Blessed is He Who spoke and the* OLAM *came into being* to *Unique One, the Life-Force of the* OLAMIM is also understandable. The earlier part of *Baruch She'Amar*, lacking as it does the *You*, speaks of the Ribbono shel Olam functioning in a world that is absolutely hidden from us. In that world, there are no divisions between the world of the idea and the world of the physical reality. All is one, one *olam*. However, the next part of *Baruch She'Amar* is intro-duced by its own blessing, structured—as we have learned to expect—with its own *You*. That is the world within which we function, even as we accept that other worlds beyond our ken exist. Although we cannot experience these worlds, we know that they exist. From that vantage point, it is appropriate to refer to God as *the Life-Force of the* OLAMIM.

Chapter 3. Building a Sanctuary

1. Upon reflection, it seems possible that Sforno saw Sotah 9a, זה משה ודוד שלא שלטו שונאיהם במעשיהם, as a source.

2. See appendix to this chapter for a treatment of one of the issues which this passage raises.

3. Here is a Midrash which gives body to our formulation:

משל למלך שהיה לו בת יחידה בא אחד מן המלכים ונטלה ביקש לילך לו לארצו וליטול לאשתו אמר לו בתי שנתתי לך יחידית היא, לפרוש ממנה איני יכול, לומר לך אל תטלה איני יכול לפי שהיא אשתך אלא זו טובה עשה לי שכל מקום שאתה הולך קיטון אחד עשה לי שאדור אצלכם שאיני יכול להניח את בתי, כך אמר הקדוש ברוך הוא לישראל נתתי לכם את התורה לפרוש הימנה איני יכול, לומר לכם אל תטלוה איני יכול אלא בכל מקום שאתם הולכים בית אחד עשו לי שאדור בתוכו שנאמר ועשו לי מקדש.

[God's command that we build a Mishkan] can be illustrated by the story of a king who had an only daughter. A royal suitor took her as a wife. Eventually he decided that the time had come to return home.

The king said to him, "Your wife is my only daughter. I do not have it in me to part from her. I realize that I cannot keep you here. Please do me a favor. Make a small room wherever you should find yourself so that I can always be close to my daughter."

Chapter 4. Somber Intimations

1. See *Chovos HaLevavos, Sha'ar HaPerishus*, Chapter 4.

2. I am assuming that Shlomo HaMelech knew, but the people did not, that this Beis HaMikdash would not last forever. I may be wrong in this. I have no source but just assume that the people would not have been able to celebrate as wholeheartedly as they did if they knew the truth.

3. It would be interesting to know the source of Rambam's asser-tion. That is, of course, not the same thing as asking why it was a foregone conclusion that indeed the Beis HaMikdash would one day be destroyed. It is to this second issue that the next part of this essay will be devoted. In the meantime, we are back at our problem. What is the source for this assertion?

My electronic library—while showing that both Rashi and Radak in their commentaries on TaNaCh also knew of this tradi-tion—pointed to only one Tannaic source: the Mechilta d'R. Shimon

NOTES

ben Yochai 18:27. It tells the story of how Yirmeyahu was sent to the Rechabites, telling them that it was the wish of the Ribbono shel Olam that they should drink wine. They refused, citing their father's command that they abstain from all wine as a sign of mourning for the Beis HaMikdash, which was eventually to be destroyed.

I doubt whether even this very specific reference can serve as a source. It seems eminently possible that at the time this conversation took place—Yirmeyahu was active in the waning years of the first Beis HaMikdash—it was obvious to everybody that the ultimate destruction was inevitable. It does not tell us that this could already have been known in the times of Shlomo HaMelech.

Radak on II Divrey HaYamim 35:3 states that there was a Rabbinic tradition that Shlomo HaMelech built the subterranean passages because it was known that the Beis HaMikdash was going to be destroyed. This is certainly reliable testimony that Rambam's assertion has a Talmudic source. However, as mentioned above, I have not been able to find this passage.

4. This requires an explanation. Rambam rules in Beis HaBechirah, Chapter 6, that *we may offer sacrifices even in the absence of the Beis HaMikdash*. His reasoning is as follows.

... לפי שקדושת המקדש וירושלים מפני השכינה ושכינה אינה בטלה, והרי הוא אומר והשמותי את מקדשיכם ואמרו חכמים אע"פ ששמומין בקדושתן הן עומדים.

Now, why do I say that the sanctity of the Beis HaMikdash and Yerushalayim was a permanent state, not affected by later conquests? . . . It is because the sanctity of the Beis Hamikdash and Yerushalayim derives from the Presence of God, and that Presence can never be curtailed.

How, then, can I write that one day God's Presence would depart? It is very clear that God's Presence did indeed depart from the Beis HaMikdash shortly before its destruction. See Rosh HaShanah 31a, which states that *God's Presence left in ten stages*. The source for this contention is the prophet Yechezkel, who hints at these stages in the first few chapters of his book. This is in fact why these sections of the book are known as the *description of the Chariot*. This because a chariot conveys a sense of movement.

In the light of this reality, we must explain Rambam's statement as meaning that although God's Presence did depart, the effect of its once having been there lasts permanently.

This is something that we have to keep in mind throughout the coming chapters. When we talk about the impermanence of Shlomo HaMelech's Beis HaMikdash, we refer only to the building. But the Presence of God, which descended during the inaugural celebrations, would leave its mark forever.

176

5. Of course, this provides a justification but not a reason for
Shlomo's interest in involving Chiram. The interested reader might
wish to consult Section Two, Chapter 2, of my ArtScroll Divrey
HaYamim, vol. 2.

Chapter 5. The Episode of the Spies Revisited

1. Sforno's ideas are shared by other Rishonim. Thus, for example,
Rashi on Tehillim 106:27:

ולהפיל זרעם בגוים - מאותו שעה נגזר עליהם חורבן הבית שהרי ליל ט' באב בכו ואמר
הקב"ה הם בכו בכיה של חנם ואני אקבע להם בכיה לדורות.

"To cast their offspring among the nations." From that moment, the
destruction of the Beis HaMikdash was decreed, for on the night
of Tish'ah B'Av they wept, so the Holy One, blessed be He, said,
"Since they cried for nothing, I will give them a reason to cry for
generations."

2. Not just give them knowledge of the land.

3. Not, as implied by the absence of the word in Shlach, that at this
time there will be no real inheritance.

4. In coming chapters, we will be returning to this comment by
Rashi many times. On the words *Come and inherit the land*, he comments *You will need no weapons*.

5. In an earlier draft of this chapter, I attempted to explain why the
Shlach passage chooses one of the two possible formulations while
the Devarim passage chooses the other. This is no idle question,
and certainly deserves a great deal of thought. In the end, however,
I decided that such an explanation would take us too far away from
what really concerns us in these essays. The thoughtful reader will
certainly draw his own conclusions.

6. At this point, it would be a good idea to glance at Chapter 19.
There we show that Kaleiv, in attempting to dissuade the people
from their rebellion, used language that precisely parallels the
VaEira wording.

Chapter 6. The Spies and the Golden Calf

1. אלמלי לא נשתברו לוחות הראשונות לא נשתכחה תורה מישראל. רב אחא בר יעקב
אמר, אין כל אומה ולשון שולטת בהן—*If the first set of Tablets had not been shattered, the Jews never would have forgotten the Torah. R. Acha bar Ya'akov
said, No nation would be able to rule over them* (Eiruvin 54a).

2. Our focus in this book is the sin of the spies. Perhaps there will
be another occasion for discussing the sin of the golden calf in the
same detail.

3. I feel some ambivalence about including this section. I will present my considerations here:

We have learned within that *every calamity that the Jews suffer contains within itself some of the punishment deriving from the episode of the golden calf*. This certainly conveys the sense of a statement of fact. Every suffering to which we have been exposed through the ages contains a little of what is due to us from the sin of the golden calf.

I am not convinced that this is, in fact, so. Is it not possible that this was indeed the Ribbono shel Olam's intent when He made this statement, but that as a result of Moshe Rabbeinu's intercession, He withdrew this threat? After all, the entire drama in Ki Sissa centers around just such willingness on the part of the Ribbono shel Olam to permit Himself to be persuaded by Moshe Rabbeinu's prayers. I have tried to find the sources for Rashi's assertion (see, for example, Sanhedrin 102a) and they do not, as far as I can tell, preclude the possibility that in the end all was forgiven.

The source which, in language, is closest to Rashi's words seems to bear out my thoughts. It comes from Shemos Rabbah 43:3:

ד"א ויחל משה הה"ד (משלי כט) "אנשי לצון יפיחו קריה", אלו ישראל שנתנו פיחה בעולם בעגל שעשו, דא"ר אסי אין דור ודור שאינו נוטל אוקיא ממעשה העגל. "וחכמים ישיבו אף", זה משה שהשיב אפו של הקב"ה בסניגוריא שלמד על ישראל, הוי ויחל משה.

The passage seeks to understand the implications of the words *And Moshe petitioned*. It quotes Mishley 29:8—*Scoffers will set the town on fire*—and tells that this refers to the Israelites who brought conflagration to the world through the golden calf that they constructed. This, in accordance with R. Yose's teaching: "There is no generation that does not suffer to some extent from the sin of the golden calf." Then the verse in Mishley continues: *but the wise turn back the anger*. And this refers to Moshe Rabbeinu, who turned back the anger of the Ribbono shel Olam through his advocacy for Yisrael.

It seems to me that the simple meaning of the verse is that "the wise" turn back the evil that has been brought about by the scoffers. That is in fact how the Vilna Gaon explains the verse in his commentary on Mishley, if I understand him correctly. If that is so, then R. Yose's statement about each generation being punished in part for the sin of the golden calf was not meant to describe what actually was but what might have been. Moshe Rabbeinu's prayer may well have changed everything.

If all this is true, this section does not really belong here. However, it is my impression that it is generally accepted that in fact we are all still suffering from the sin of the golden calf. Moreover, this seems borne out by Rashi a little later on at 14:33. I ask your indulgence, dear reader, for my ambivalence.

4. I have used Mesorah Publications' Stone Chumash for this translation.

5. It is important to grasp the implications of this devastating phrase. The Ribbono shel Olam is saying, "From My point of view, there is really no reason to continue. My dreams for the whole world raised to sanctity by a Chosen People have been shattered along with the Tablets. What possible purpose can there be in bringing these people into Eretz Yisrael without a Torah? Let them go to *where I have told you.* I permit this as a favor to you, in your honor. It has nothing to do with My original plans. It is not the *land of the Hittites and Emorites* of which I spoke to Avraham. It is an anonymous place in which these now anonymous people can build their state. I will have no more interest in it than I have in any of the surrounding countries."

6. How we understand these words of Ramban depends upon the discussion in endnote 3. I suggest that you, dear reader, look it over once more. We know from *Ki Sissa* that in the end, as a result of Moshe Rabbeinu's prayers, the Ribbono shel Olam *did* forgive the sin of the golden calf. That given, we can understand Ramban here in one of two ways. Either he means precisely what he seems to mean, that in fact the Ribbono shel Olam *at this stage* did not forgive and that, indeed, when ultimately Moshe Rabbeinu elicited atonement this verse became irrelevant. Or we will have to assume that when Ramban says that the Ribbono shel Olam will not forgive, it means only relative to the *day of accounting.* The punishments will continue although the sin, as such, will have been forgiven.

7. See previous note.

8. See Ramban, Devarim 9:8: והוכיח אותם בעונות אשר גרמו להם רעה **ולא נמחלו**, והזכיר להם **ענין המרגלים** ומי מריבה—*He rebuked them for the sins that had caused them such harm and for which they had not been forgiven, and mentioned the episodes of the spies and of the waters of Merivah.*

9. We will not get into a detailed description here of why the sin of the golden calf might be considered inadvertent. It is likely that the answer resides in any one of the apologetics that are offered by various commentators in order to soften the horror of that transgression. Of these, Kuzari 1:97 may be considered to be representative.

From Ramban, it is clear that no similar defense is possible for the spies.

10. The words *I have forgiven according to your words* play a major role in our Selichos prayers. Many *piyyutim* are structured around them and they are constantly invoked to elicit God's forgiveness. We seem to be praying that just as in the past He forgave us as a result of our words, so should He do now.

I find this usage particularly strange in consideration of the fact that, as we demonstrate above, this expression is used to denote a *limitation* of the Ribbono shel Olam's willingness to accede to Moshe Rabbeinu's prayer, rather than to portray a generous willingness to eradicate the past.

11. At this point, I recommend a careful study of Ramban on Devarim 32:26. He demonstrates that even this argument and others like it can open the floodgates of the Ribbono shel Olam's mercy.

Chapter 7. Heresy

1. As I reread this chapter, I am struck by something which I did not notice earlier. Why does Moshe Rabbeinu change the more passive *come* to the more intense *go up?*

Perhaps we have here an example of Moshe Rabbeinu's greatness as a leader. It is true that when the Ribbono shel Olam had spoken to him, He had said *Come and possess it*, as reported earlier. From the Ribbono shel Olam's perspective, the people would be passive. He would bring them in and they would have nothing to do but follow. Here Moshe Rabbeinu tells them that while it is true that from an objective standpoint they will be passive, it is also true that they were where they were because of their own merit. In a sense they are "going up." Moshe Rabbeinu is saying, "Believe in yourselves!"

Chapter 8. An Introduction to
Our Analysis of the Parashas HaMeraglim

1. Ramban's argument with Rashi is not limited to the Shlach phrase שלך לך. They disagreed on the same issue in BeReishis 12:1, לך לך, and in Shemos 34:1, פסל לך.

2. בדרך שאדם רוצה לילך מוליכין אותו (Makkos 10b).

Chapter 9. Moments That Move Our History

1. See Foreword. As established there, we are assuming Ramban's second offering.

2. I owe this part of the essay to HaRav Ya'akov Kamenetzky in his *Iyyunim BaMikra.*

3. I note the following textual oddity because it seems to affirm Ramban's assertion.

When, in Shemos 3, the Ribbono shel Olam tells Moshe Rabbeinu of His plans for the Israelites, He uses the following language:

וארד להצילו מיד מצרים ולהעלותו מן הארץ ההוא אל ארץ טובה ורחבה אל ארץ זבת חלב ודבש אל **מקום הכנעני** והחתי והאמורי והפריזי והחוי והיבוסי.

And I will descend to save [the Jewish nation] from the hand of Egypt, and to raise it from that land to a land that is good and broad, to a land flowing with milk and honey, to *the place of the Canaanites* and the Hittites and the Emorites and the Perizzites and the Hivvites and the Jebusites.

The Ribbono shel Olam promises to bring us to the PLACE *of the Canaanites*, not the LAND *of the Canaanites*. As far as I can see from my electronic library, this is one of the four times in TaNaCh in which the word *place* is used in this sense. People in TaNaCh usually occupy *lands*, not *places*. *Place* is generally used instead to refer to the location of objects: *the place of the altar, the place of the ark*, and so on. These objects are "placed" there—they do not dwell there.

This usage would tend to support Ramban's claim that the Canaanites did not really belong in Eretz Canaan in the sense that it was the land that had been assigned to them. They were there only as Shem's slaves. Eretz Canaan was the land in which they were "placed" temporarily, not one in which they were to dwell eternally.

I believe that this linguistic insight has merit, and I have therefore recorded it. There are, however, two problems that, as of this moment, I have been unable to solve.

The first is that Ramban himself, similarly taking note of the unusual use of *place*, offers a different explanation. He believes that the term is used here to underline that when the Israelites enter Eretz Caanan, it will be their *exclusive* place—they will not dwell "among" the Canaanites as their forefathers had done. If my interpretation of *place* had merit, one would certainly expect Ramban to use it here.

Secondly, there is the language that the Ribbono shel Olam uses in verse 17, where He tells Moshe Rabbeinu what to say to the Israelites. Here is the verse:

ואמר אעלה אתכם מעני מצרים אל ארץ הכנעני והחתי. . . .

I declare that I will lift you from the torment of Egypt to the LAND OF THE CANAANITES *and the Hittites. . . .*

Why here does the Ribbono shel Olam change the *place* that He had used earlier into *land*? This change appears to offer an excuse on behalf of the Jews when they rejected the Ribbono shel Olam's invitation to simply walk into the land. As we have argued above, this option existed only because, in fact, the Canaanites had no real rights to the land and were only there as slaves with the task of preparing the land for Shem's descendants. But although this was something that Moshe Rabbeinu knew (*place*), the people did not.

Chapter 10. Rejection on a Large Scale

1. I say *perhaps more tragic* advisedly. Before I began work on this book, I would, I suppose, have been certain that the second was the worse of the two. The first, so I would have argued, was a regrettable

NOTES

lack of faith but was in no way comparable to the second, which resulted in so many tragedies. But now that we have analyzed the first
one in depth, I am not so certain. In fact, if pressed, I would probably
opt for the first.

2. See Yalkut Shimoni, II Shmuel 151.

3. My good friend R. Ilan Feldman of Atlanta pointed out the following: the following passage from Ta'anis 29a is well known:

אמר רבה אמר רבי יוחנן: אותה לילה ליל תשעה באב היה. אמר להם הקדוש ברוך הוא
אתם בכיתם בכיה של חנם, ואני קובע לכם בכיה לדורות.

That night [when the people wept because of the spies' report] was
Tish'ah B'Av. God said to them, "On this night you wept *chinam*
(literally, "free"). I will make this into a night of tears throughout
your exile."

What, precisely, does *chinam* mean? If it simply connotes *without
reason*, it would appear to be inappropriate in this case. The people
were afraid, and from that standpoint they had every reason to weep.
One can argue with their theology but not with their emotions.

R. Ilan suggested that *chinam* implies *a weeping that does not impose
any responsibilities*. It describes a state of mind in which there seems to
be absolutely no way out of the dilemma. Because there is nothing
that I can do, I am not challenged to do anything.

Let us appoint a leader and return to Egypt can be said only by people
who have given up all hope.

4. I use the term *sober judgment* to contrast what happened here
with the emotional grumbling in the earlier two cases. However, it
is not clear to me how the Jews could have imagined making their
way back to Egypt without the protective Clouds of Glory or the
miraculous well and manna. All these, one would certainly suppose,
would have disappeared had their rebellion against the Ribbono
shel Olam actually taken place.

If they assumed that these would continue even under the leadership of the newly minted idol or the usurping Dasan and Aviram,
then there are dimensions to these stories that I am not capable of
plumbing.

5. In the final year of their desert wanderings, when the people
grumbled about the lack of water after Miriam's death, Moshe and
Aharon also prostrated themselves (BeMidbar 20:6). However, it
is worthy of note that there the language is not, as it is here, *before the
entire nation of Israel*.

The late Rav Joseph B. Soloveitchik, *zatzal*, explains what
happened there as follows: Moshe and Aharon gave way to that
gesture of despair because the people's grumbling on that occasion
was immeasurably more devastating than anything that had gone

NOTES

before. All the earlier disappointments had taken place in the first two years—that is, while the Jews who had left Egypt were the main players. Their obstreperousness was understandable and excusable. They were a slave people, only recently worshipping idols in Egypt, with very little conception of what a relationship to the Ribbono shel Olam would entail. It was easy for them to feel frustrated when things did not work out as they had expected. But the grumbling in the fortieth year was different. The old, erstwhile slaves had already died out. The people were all students of Moshe Rabbeinu who had either been born or grown into adulthood under his tutelage. The realization that these, his disciples, had learned nothing at all, that they were complaining in precisely the same way their parents had done, must have been totally devastating to Moshe Rabbeinu. He went to the Tent of Meeting and prostrated himself before God in utter despair.

Obviously, none of this is applicable to the story of the spies.

6. It is interesting to note the singular *and he fell* instead of the plural *and they fell* that might be expected. It seems that the initiative for this act of submission to the people's will came from Moshe Rabbeinu alone, and Aharon just followed suit. Perhaps, since the issue was one of leadership rather than of representation of the Jews in the sacrificial service, this is understandable.

Chapter 11. Stalking the Truth Lurking Beneath the Facts

1. The centrality of rebellion is confirmed in the Torah's account of the spies. See BeMidbar 14:9, אך בה' אל תמרדו—*but at least do not rebel against HaShem*—and Devarim 1:26.

2. This dating can be of major significance to us when we think about the dynamics of repentance. We are used to viewing the fulfillment of the self-examination to which Rosh HaShanah stimulates us as having its expression in Yom Kippur, the culmination of the Ten Days of Repentance. But in the Nechemiah passage, we see the coupling of the awe of Rosh HaShanah with the rejoicing of Succos, and they together provide the impetus for the confession that we are analyzing.

3. I cannot offer any explanation for the fact that Tehillim 106 makes reference to the story of Korach (verse 17) out of its chronological order.

4. The verse in Shlach that we have quoted in endnote 1 points to a rebellion against God. Still, we have some more refining to do. We will attempt this in the next chapter.

183

Chapter 12. The Lure of the Ordinary

1. I am not sure how much weight we should attach to this phrase. There are many sources that mention and detail the ten tests. This is the only one that makes the claim that the sin of the spies was the worst of all. Still, as far as I know, there is no reason to doubt that this is an authentic reading.

2. Ramban explains that the phrase אל בני ישראל, *to the Children of Israel*, indicates that the spies told this to the people but not in the presence of Moshe and Aharon. The sequence of events was as follows:

The spies returned and reported on all the issues that they had been asked to investigate except for two of them. They said nothing of whether the land was "good" or "bad," or of whether the people were "few" or "many." They kept these two matters in reserve so that if their original strategy did not work, they could fall back on these.

Initially they said nothing about these matters because they thought it would be enough simply to stress the strategic problems. The people were too strong, the cities too well protected. This, however, did not work as they had hoped, because Kaleiv persuaded the people that they really had nothing to fear (verse 30).

The spies now had to resort to bald lies. These, however, they were afraid to tell in the presence of Moshe and Aharon, and therefore they waited until Moshe and Aharon had left. They then followed the people into their tents and slandered the land, as we shall discuss within.

3. He notes the difference between the verb that our verse uses, *they* BROUGHT OUT *evil reports against the land,* and the verb that the Torah uses in describing Yosef's talebearing to his father, *and Yosef* BROUGHT *their evil slander* (BeReishis 37:2). The former is used when the slander is false and the latter when it is true.

4. Here is what Kuzari writes at 2:62:

כבר אמרתי לך כי השכינה היתה בישראל במדרגת הרוח בגוף האדם. מועילה אותם החיות האלהית ונותנת להם זיו והדר בגופתם ובתכונותם ובמשכניהם. ובעת שמתרחקת מהם מסתכלת עצתם ויבערו גופיהם וישתנה יפים.

I have already told you that God's Presence was in the midst of the Jews as the soul is within the body. That divine life-force helps them *and gives them radiance and beauty in their bodies and in their make-up and in their dwelling places.* And when it grows distant from them, their intelligence fails and their bodies grow coarse and their beauty fades.

5. See Ibn Ezra to this verse.

6. See appendix to this chapter.

7. The phrase comes from Yechezkel 20:35. See Malbim there.

Chapter 13. The Spies and the Golden Calf Revisited

1. Rashi renders the word תרוכין, *t'ruchin*. This word, in this form, is familiar to us from the text of a divorce decree, which contains the phrase *a scroll of* t'ruchin, *sending away*. The Aramaic Targum renders ואשיצינון, *v'ashitzinun, I will make them leave.* ([א]שיצא is the שפעל form of יצא, *to go out*.)

2. Here is Maharal on this Rashi:

וא"ת, אדרבא זהו כסא של ארבע רגלים . . . ואין זה קשיא . . . וכאשר אמר למשה

ואעשך לגוי גדול רצה שהוא יהיה משה האב לאומה . . . ולא יהיו נקראים על שם

האבות, כמו שנוח לא יקרא אב לישראל אע"ג שכל ישראל יצאו ממנו, וכן שם לא נקרא

אב, שלא נקרא אבות לישראל אלא אברהם יצחק ויעקב, כך לא יהיה נקרא אב אלא

משה שהוא נעשה לגוי גדול.

And if you say: on the contrary, this would be a four-legged stool . . . that is no difficulty. . . . When God told Moshe, "I will make you into a great nation," He intended that Moshe would be the father of the nation . . . and they would not be connected to the patriarchs, just as No'ach isn't called the father of Israel even though every Jew is his offspring, nor is Shem called the father of Israel. The only patriarchs of Israel are Avraham, Yitzchak and Ya'akov. Thus, only Moshe would be called the patriarch and made into a great nation.

3. There is, of course, the possibility that since Moshe Rabbeinu had rejected this possibility with the metaphor of the two stools, this option was not viable anymore.

4. For a fuller treatment of this Midrash, you, dear reader, might want to look at the Introduction to Sefer BeMidbar in the Netziv's commentary on Chumash. Here we will deal with this Midrash only to the extent that it affects the thesis we are attempting to develop.

We should just note that those who left Egypt are described as "light" because they were led by Moshe Rabbeinu (who is compared to the sun). Those who were to enter the land are the generation of relative "darkness," because they would be led by Yehoshua (who is compared to the moon).

5. See Shabbos 116a. The passage there is more complicated than we have indicated here. But for our purposes, our somewhat simplified account suffices.

6. I am referring to the original impetus to send the spies. Later, when these returned, there were, of course, the sins of speaking and believing slander.

7. And still R. Akiva in Sanhedrin 108a and 110b holds that the generation of the wilderness has no portion in the world-to-come. See Chapter 14 for a detailed discussion of this issue.

See also Devarim 9:23, where the Torah, in regard to the spies, says that the Jews *rebelled against the mouth of HaShem your God and did not believe in Him and did not heed His voice.* However, all this may refer to the Jews' determination to return to Egypt rather than to their initial wish to send the spies.

Chapter 14. The Tragedy of the Generation of the Wilderness

1. See Rashi, Ta'anis 30b: כל ארבעים שנה שהיו במדבר, בכל ערב תשעה באב היה הכרוז יוצא ואומרת "צאו לחפור" והיה כל אחד ואחד יוצא וחופר לו קבר וישן בו. ולמחר הכרוז יוצא וקרא, "יבדלו החיים מן המתים."—*The entire forty years that they were in the wilderness, every Tish'ah B'Av eve, a proclamation would declare, "Come forth to dig," and every individual would come out and dig a grave and lie in it.... The next day a proclamation would declare, "Separate the living from the dead...."*

Immediately after the story of the spies, we have Korach's rebellion. After that, the Torah goes straight to Chukkas and the events that took place in the fortieth year. Concerning the intervening thirty-eight years, we know nothing at all. It would seem that during that period, nothing happened that in any way needed to be immortalized.

Why is the story of the fortieth year prefaced by the description of the red heifer? The late Rav Joseph B. Soloveitchik explains that the pervasive reality during that period was nothing but death and dying. The red heifer posits an ability to free oneself from the cloying spiritual paralysis of uncleanness caused by death.

2. I have chosen to quote the Talmud instead of the Mishnah on 107b, because the Talmud is more wide-ranging in its discussion.

3. My translation is an attempt to capture Rashi's commentary on Tehillim. I imagine that in the context of the Talmud we will need to take *tranquillity* as a name for the world-to-come.

4. See Shemos 24:5.

5. This is a particularly apt translation of the original Aramaic. I borrowed it from the ArtScroll Sanhedrin.

6. I am aware that the possibility exists that the Ribbono shel Olam will apportion His rewards and punishments in accordance with the determination of the Sages of Israel, in the same way that their opinion is what determines the status of uncleanness or purity in regards to some forms of plague even if that opinion flies in the face of what the Ribbono shel Olam Himself felt to be the halachah (Bava Metzia 86a).

Still, I believe that there are major differences between the issues. The Ribbono shel Olam gave us the Torah with absolute authority to interpret it as seemed best to us. *It is not in the heavens.* That, however, may well apply only to matters of halachah as they concern *us*.

After all, even though *He has given the earth to human beings*, nevertheless, *the heavens are the heavens of HaShem*.

7. One example is the word for "moon." TaNaCh knows only *yare'ach*, whereas the Mishnah uses only *levanah*.

8. We all know Tehillim 95 as the *L'chu n'ranena* of Friday night. As so often happens to most of us, familiarity breeds superficiality and few of us are troubled by the strange structure of this psalm. There seems to be no connection at all between the opening verses and the final four. We cannot, in the context of this essay, analyze the entire psalm. I recommend to the interested reader that he study R. Shamshon Refael Hirsch's commentary on Psalms. As so often happens, R. Hirsch makes it all logical and simple.

9. I have put the word *warriors*—my translation of *anshey milchamah*—into quotes for the following reason. Rashi says simply that these were men *from twenty years old who served in the army*. Now Rashi is explaining only what this expression means in the present context; he does not offer a reason for the choice of this particular term. It does not occur in either the Shlach or the Devarim account of the spies. Why use it here?

With some degree of diffidence, since I have not found my idea in any of the commentators, I suggest the following: We have seen throughout our discussion that the people's request that spies be sent was a rejection of the Ribbono shel Olam's offer that they would enter Eretz Yisrael as honored owners, without having to fight for it at all. In demanding that spies be sent, the people opted for a natural and prospectively warlike, rather than a miraculous, entry into the land. This is why the Torah calls them *warriors* with a deep sigh. And as long as these men, who had so gravely misunderstood their destiny, remained alive, the affection implied in the verb *speak* was inappropriate.

Chapter 15. A World Beneath The World

1. See Rashi on BeReishis 11:32.

2. Six hundred leaders of thousands; six thousand leaders of hundreds; twelve thousand leaders of fifty and sixty thousand leaders of ten.

3. *His men.*

4. Among other objections, he raises the issue of the census that was taken later on. If, indeed, so many had been killed, that should have been reflected in the numbers.

5. הבועל ארמית קנאין פוגעין בו.

6. See Sanhedrin 45a. Ramban's statement accords with the opinion of R. Eliezer.

7. The prefix ל can of course have many different meanings. Perhaps we might render *for God's sake* and so on.

8. Maharal makes this point in *Gur Aryeh*. Stoning usually takes place *outside the camp*, far away from prying eyes. Here the Torah insists that the hanging was supposed to be done within the encampment, publicly for all to see.

9. See Rashi. He cites a well-known parable: The king's twin was a robber. He was caught and hanged upon the gibbet. Because the twins looked alike, passersby might have thought that it was the king who was hanging.

10. Our understanding of *before HaShem* as a means of avoiding the desecration of God's Name can also explain the Shmuel passage that we quote above. Sha'ul's descendants were to be hanged in order to eliminate the desecration of God's Name brought about by the slaughter of the Kohanic city of Nov.

11. לתקן עולם במלכות שדי.

Chapter 16. Meeting Yehoshua and Kaleiv

1. See Chapter 13.

2. Megillah 13b.

3. ויתנו להם הנשים אשר חיו מנשי יבש גלעד.

4. Rashi suggests that the verse conveys the idea that Yehoshua and Kaleiv were given those portions of the land that would otherwise have gone to the other ten spies.

I am not certain whether Rashi means this as the simple meaning of the text.

Chapter 17. Kaleiv I

1. See Rashi at 13:16. Rashi is quoting Sotah 34b. Most of the major commentators feel that the simple meaning of the words does not demand this interpretation. Reference to the change of name may simply serve to answer the question of how the Hoshe'a of verse 9 becomes Yehoshua in the rest of the story. His birth name was certainly Hoshe'a. However, when Moshe Rabbeinu took him as his personal servant, he changed his name to Yehoshua. It was customary in those days to assign someone a new name when he undertook a new position.

2. See Rashi on 13:22. This explanation, also taken from Sotah 34b, is based upon the change from the plural *they went up* to the singular *he came*. It certainly seems borne out by Devarim 1:36, Shoftim 1:20 and the Yehoshua passage that we are about to examine. Nevertheless, the commentators point out that the singular *he came* could also mean: *Each member of the group of spies came to Chevron.*

3. We will be discussing this episode in depth in Chapter 19.

NOTES

Chapter 18. Kaleiv II

1. In 4:5 we read, *Ashchur Avi Teko'a had two wives, Chel'ah and Na'arah.* We will see below that Ashchur Avi Teko'a is Kaleiv. The two women whom he married are really two names for Miriam: Chel'ah (*ill*) and Na'arah (*young*), because as a result of Kaleiv's loving care she not only was cured but actually returned to her youthful bloom.

2. The name, derived from the root *parah, to bear fruit,* is appropriate, since it was through Miriam and her mother, Yocheved, when these two were midwives in Pharaoh's Egypt, that the Jews were able to be fruitful and multiply (Tanchuma, Ki Sissa).

3. At the literal level, the meaning is that he was born in the area known as Efras (Rashi).

4. This Divrey HaYamim passage refers to *Kaleiv the son of Chetzron,* not *Kaleiv the son of Yefunneh* (as our Kaleiv is introduced in Shlach). Commentators deal with this issue in various ways. For our purposes, it is sufficient to note that the Midrashim with which we are dealing take it as given that the reference is to Kaleiv the son of Yefunneh.

   The source for this loving, fatherlike devotion is as follows. At 4:5 we learn that Ashchur Avi Teko'a had two wives. Further along we will see that the "two" wives were really two names for Miriam, and also that Ashchur Avi Teko'a refers to Kaleiv. The Talmud explains the "Avi" of that name by saying that in marrying her, Kaleiv became like a *father* to Miriam. Rashi explains that he provided her with nourishing food and medicines to help her over her sickness.

5. Some others are: Yesher (*to be straight*) because he preserved his integrity; Shovav (*to be rebellious*) because he had the courage to rebel against the spies; Ardon (*to control*) because he was able to control his inclination to throw in his lot with the spies; and Teko'a (*to fasten*) because he cleaved to God.

Chapter 19. Kaleiv III

1. It is interesting that in English the verb *to want* means both *to desire,* as it does in the Holy Tongue, and also to be *in need of something.* "For want of a nail the shoe was lost." Desire is the child of lack, and lack is something that we do not associate with the Ribbono shel Olam.

2. At this point, it would be useful to study Ramban on BeReishis 12:10 carefully. He deals with our Sages' teaching that the Ribbono shel Olam had told Avraham, *Go out and prepare the way before your offspring.*

Chapter 20. Kaleiv IV

1. Rashi is not completely clear. He writes, *He is wounded by our sins and beaten down by our transgressions*, but does not suggest how this came about. Kuzari 2:44 thinks that the words imply an assimilation of foreign values. Based upon Tehillim 106:35, he maintains that, in the course of our exile, we learned to act as did our host nations.

2. I found it particularly difficult to translate these verses. I have borrowed some phrases from the English translation of the Jewish Publication Society of America.

By quoting only some of the verses in this extraordinarily difficult passage, I have avoided having to deal with some of the surprising assumptions that it seems to make. The commentators approach the passage from different angles. For a full treatment, I would advise the reader to study Kuzari, part of which I referenced in the previous endnote.

Chapter 21. When Leopards Change Their Spots

1. The singular יהיה instead of the expected plural יהיו persuades me that the subject is the sorrow which suffused all these days, rather than the days themselves.

2. For this translation, I have borrowed from the Jewish Publication Society's translation.

3. Once more, I owe much of this translation to the Jewish Publication Society. The interpretation of the latter part of the sentence follows Radak, rather than Rashi.

Appendix to Chapter 3

1. See Ramban, Shemos 40:34:

"And the cloud covered the Tent of Meeting." This tells us that the cloud would surround the Tent and conceal it.

"And the glory of Hashem filled the Mishkan." It was filled with the Glory, which dwelt within the cloud that was in the Mishkan. [This is similar to the situation at Mt. Sinai, where we learn of] "the dark cloud where God was" (Shemos 20:17).

The verse tells us that Moshe could not even come to the entrance of the Tent of Meeting because the cloud covered it. [For one thing,] Moshe did not have permission to enter the cloud. And in addition, how could he enter the Mishkan, since it was filled with the Glory of Hashem?

The purpose was that he not enter without permission. He first had to be summoned before going into the cloud—just as had occurred at Mt. Sinai, when God "called to Moshe on the seventh day from within the cloud" (Shemos 24:16), following which "Moshe went into the cloud" (ibid. 18).

In simple terms, we see from the fact that "Hashem spoke to [Moshe] from the tent of meeting" (Vayikra 1:1) that Moshe did not [initially] enter the Mishkan. Rather, God summoned Moshe from the Tent of Meeting. Moshe then stood at the entrance of the Tent of Meeting and God spoke to him.

2. When we say that Moshe Rabbeinu was not involved with the individual artifacts, we mean only that he did not take part in their construction. However, the Midrash points out that the Mishkan will always be associated with Moshe because he was so deeply involved in making sure that everything was done correctly. Here is a part of the Midrash:

Moshe went to the craftsmen every day and throughout the day to teach them how to do the work flawlessly. The Holy One, blessed be He, had told Moshe, "See to it that you make [the artifacts] according to their [proper] form." And indeed the workers made "every single thing, just as Hashem had commanded Moshe." They were careful with "every single thing" because Moshe was always there.

Then "Moshe saw all of the work . . . and Moshe blessed them." What blessing did he give them? He said, "May the pleasantness of Hashem our God . . ." (Tehillim 90)—meaning, "May God's Presence dwell upon the work of your hands."

R. Chiya bar Yosef taught the following:

During the seven days of the inauguration, Moshe set up the Mishkan and took it apart twice a day. Do not think that any Levite helped him—that is not the case. Rather, as our Sages teach, he would set it up and take it apart without anyone's help. We see this from the fact that the verse speaks of "the day that Moshe *completed*," rather than "the day that Moshe *set up*." This implies that every day he himself set it up and took it apart, at last completing this labor on the final day.

And because of Moshe's intimate involvement with this process, the Mishkan is linked to his name. Thus, the verse states, "When *Moshe* completed."

Appendix to Chapter 6

1. It is not clear to me why Ramban quotes the Yehoshua verse and not the verses in the Torah where Moshe Rabbeinu's prayers are often based on the consideration of *why should the nations say . . .*, which seems to carry the same connotation.

2. See Ramban to Devarim 32:26 where he discusses in detail the meaning of passages such as these.

IN RECOGNITION OF A

GENEROUS CONTRIBUTION

IN MEMORY

OF

Dr. Richard

&

Regina Weinberger

OF

VIENNA, AUSTRIA

&

BALTIMORE, MARYLAND

IN LOVING MEMORY

OF

Solomon Ralph

Bijou

FROM

HIS WIFE, CHILDREN,

GRANDCHILDREN

AND

GREAT-GRANDCHILDREN

IN LOVING MEMORY

OF

Esther

AND

Isaac Mezrahi

IN LOVING MEMORY

OF

Ezra & Zekia Shasho

AND

Frieda Kredy

מציבים אנו בזה

מזכרת נצח

לאבינו מורנו היקר

ר' לטמן

בן ר' חיים דוב בער ז"ל

איש צנוע

שכל חייו רץ כצבי

לעשות רצון אבינו שבשמים

ולאמנו מורתנו היקרה

רות רבקה לאה

בת ר' אברהם ע"ה

יהא זכרם ברוך

IN LOVING MEMORY

OF MY BELOVED PARENTS,

AND MORE,

MY GOOD AND PRECIOUS FRIENDS

Jack & Jeanette

Feldman

THEY WERE GENEROUS, WARMHEARTED,

AND GENTLE

YOU COULD NOT MEET THEM

WITHOUT BEING TOUCHED BY THEIR

GOODNESS

WITH A SMILE ON HIS WISE FACE

AND NOVHARDOK MUSSAR IN HIS HEART

HaRav

Chaim Mordechai

Weinkrantz זצ"ל

UNDERSTOOD US ALL SO WELL, SO VERY WELL,

NO PROBLEM BUT HIS WISDOM FOUND A SOLUTION.

NO PAIN BUT HIS EMPATHY WAS A HEALING BALM.

CHILD OF A CULTURE VERY DIFFERENT FROM

OUR OWN, HE NEVERTHELESS FOUND

COMMONALITY IN HIS AND OUR JEWISH HEARTS.

WE WILL NEVER FORGET THE BOOKS WHICH HE

SO DILIGENTLY TAUGHT US NOR THE LIFE LESSONS

FOR WHICH HE WAS A LIVING TEXT.

—THE MONDAY SHIUR

WELCOME

TO

LITTLE

Moshe

AND

HIS SWEET CUDDLY COUSIN

Rachelle Bracha

WE ARE ALL

JUST AS HAPPY AND GRATEFUL

TO GOD

AS WE CAN BE

—SABA AND SAVTA